The Growth Marketer's Playbook

The Growth Marketer's Playbook

A Strategic Guide to Growing Your Business in Today's Digital World

JIM HUFFMAN

Contents

Dedication

For all overworked founders and under-appreciated marketers.

Introduction

Thank you for purchasing The Growth Marketer's Playbook. My goal is to share with you everything I have learned growing startups. Before we start, I want to cut to the chase. I have created a lot of free materials for you. They can be found at growthmarketersplaybook.com/resources/. Here you will find the exact growth templates my growth teams use, 100 growth marketing tactics, a growth reporting template and growth management tool.

Go to growthmarketersplaybook.com/resources/ to get your free resources and I hope you enjoy the book.

1. Why Growth Marketing Matters

"Growth is never by mere chance; it is the result of forces working together." —James Cash Penney, Founder of JCPenney

It doesn't matter that my business idea wasn't perfect.

The main thing is, I made it happen. It was 2011 and I built the website myself. No coders. No agency.

To clarify, it was just a simple WordPress site with some plug-ins, but to me it was a thing of beauty. It was about to change the world. And my website was live!

Damn, was I wrong.

Sadly, this is where that story ends. That finished product was the main highlight. The users never arrived. Investors never called. We never filed an IPO. Today, the domain is just a tombstone inside my GoDaddy graveyard. #RIP

Since then, I have grown four startups that generate over a million dollars in sales per month. I've mentored founders who've worked at Google, Apple and Techstars on growth and led growth marketing workshops at companies like Mattel, FedEx, Oreo, Clorox and more. I have helped market a launch of a Netflix special in over 130 countries.

As I write this book, I am running growth for an e-commerce brand that's grown from 500 subscribers and $10,000 a month to over 75,000 paying customers and seven figures in sales per month.

I haven't done this with one trick or tactic. I don't have a magic SEO hack that will change your life. I've used various channels, including search engine optimization (SEO), email marketing, referral marketing and paid social ads to drive growth. It's the principles of growth that got me to this point. That is what I hope to pass on to you through this book.

But, first, why did my first product fail, you ask?

Why didn't my website get traffic? The truth is that it never stood a chance. Connecting potential customers to the product was never a part of the strategy or my vision. Building a thoughtful acquisition strategy was not a priority. I was naive and just assumed that customers would magically appear after I built a shiny website.

It didn't fail because of the idea. It failed because I undervalued the importance of connecting my product to a market that would care about it.

In most startups, the problem isn't the product or the service you offer, it's the distribution strategy. In other words, **I didn't build a product with growth in mind.**

Unfortunately, this isn't uncommon. You might have a decent business idea bouncing around in your head. Then you muster up the energy and the team to execute on it and turn it into a workable prototype. Congrats, you have a working web app! Your mom will be proud. What's next?

How do you connect your new product with the world? Did you assume that simply because you took the initiative to make something, people will flock to it?

The truth is, this is how most people approach marketing. They put their growth strategy on the backburner. They assume that because they're building the greatest thing since the iPhone, marketing will take care of itself.

Don't get me wrong: The most important thing is a product that truly solves a problem in a way that's 10 times better than the next best solution.

But that product should also come with validated customer demand and a distribution strategy to get it in front of them. How will you connect this product with users in an organic and seamless way? Do you have a strategy other than "run Facebook ads" to acquire users?

This sounds so simple and obvious, but it's constantly forgotten. Worse, people think they're doing this, but instead they're implementing a below-average marketing and growth strategy.

Don't agree? Take it from Dave McClure, founder of 500 Startups and former head of marketing at PayPal. He says this:

"The Valley skill set that should be in highest demand and greatest scarcity is neither engineering nor design, but rather internet marketing."

How did I go from building a crappy website that barely got any users to helping startups grow to millions of dollars in sales and teaching Fortune 500 companies how to run growth? That's what we'll break down in this book, including the following topics:

- How to be customer-focused in every aspect of marketing
- How to run your growth team when it's 10 people or just you
- How to build a conversion funnel that works
- How to scale your growth strategy

- Best practices for acquiring users, converting customers and scaling growth

There is a plethora of marketing, growth-hacking and startup books out there, so how will this book actually help you? Where does this book fit in with all the other options?

First, this isn't marketing. It's growth marketing. Wait, what is growth marketing? Dave Gerhardt of Drift, a conversational marketing tool, defines growth marketing as the following, "Growth marketing is all about one thing: attracting more engaged customers. And while traditional marketing focuses on the top of the funnel, the growth marketing job description requires focusing on the entire funnel."

Said another way, marketing is about the first touchpoint and getting people to your website. Growth marketing is about the entire funnel: Getting people to the site, activating them, getting them to return and getting them to refer. The more you can control the entire experience, the more powerful you'll be as a marketer.

How is this marketing book different from all the others?

It's not about one person's growth story. It's not about high-level theories. It's about actual on-the-job advice for growing your online business. Thoughtful insight and advice along with the mistakes to avoid.

If this book was a dog it would be a mutt. A scrappy, friendly mutt named Oliver, made of the best parts of all breeds.

It's part marketing playbook (reference chapter 7).

It's part growth philosophy book (reference chapter 3).

It's part database and resources (reference chapter 9).

Plus, it has a little touch of motivation (check the last chapter).

Most importantly, this book is a resource that gives you the confidence to grow your business the right way.

It contains actionable advice and recommendations you can implement or use along every phase of your company's growth: clear examples, recommended tools and an approach for growing your website. Plus, you'll find case studies, marketing tool recommendations, 101 growth ideas to test and 11 quotes to help light a fire under your butt to get started.

This book is different because it's the stuff you actually want to know when it comes to growing your startup. Not just some academic talking high-level philosophy. It's principles and tactics.

Who am I and why should you listen to me?

I've mentioned some of my successes in growing venture-backed startups and the various workshops I teach on the subject to Fortune 500 companies. But, here is the real story about me:

I've failed more times than I've succeeded. I'm a bootstrapped startup founder who lives and dies on each day's sales. I've ridden the glorious waves of unsaturated marketing channels (think Instagram circa 2014) and I've worked with businesses that have had extreme setbacks because Google or Facebook made a "technical tweak" to their algorithm. I know how hard it can be to get one visitor to a site.

But I also know how powerful the right automated system can be for fueling your growth engine.

I've tested and implemented these principles on my students and my startups. My goal is to share all of my findings with you so you don't make the same mistakes I did. My goal is to help you expedite your growth process.

This book is for you if:

- *You have a startup idea but you don't know how to grow it.*

Great. You're halfway there. Your idea is a solution to a problem that a certain group of people have. Your growth plan is what connects your solution to those people in a scalable, repeatable and frictionless way. Right now is the perfect time to come up with a hypothesis of how you can build distribution into your product. This book will give you the tools to help determine how to grow your idea. In chapter 5, you'll learn how to uncover those opportunities.

- *You don't have a startup idea but you're working on it.*

Perfect. Now you can think about your distribution plan as you're evaluating the problem you want to solve or the product you might build. You can formulate your idea while understanding how you're going to connect with potential users that will truly value your solution. In chapter 4, you'll learn about how to know when that idea is validated and you can focus on growth.

- *You're in charge of marketing and have limited resources and no idea where to start.*

I've been there. Now is the right time to take a step back and develop your high-level plan for maximizing your time and energy. We'll dive into the right process for how you can evaluate every potential growth opportunity and then prioritize each one in order of impact and the amount of resources you will need. In chapter 7, you'll learn how to run this process yourself.

- *You don't know sh*t about marketing or growth.*

Welcome! So glad to have you here. This book will give you a framework for how to approach growth with your company, a startup or even an idea. In chapter 8, you'll get exposure to the basics of everything from Facebook ads to conversion rate optimization.

- *Your company is a rocket ship and you're wondering if you need this book.*

Congrats. Ride that wave for as long as you can but don't get a big head. This book will help you understand exactly why it's working and how to optimize your growth. In chapter 8, we talk about scaling growth by turning customers into marketers. If your growth begins to slow then we can help you determine "what to do when things get hard" and the right channels to test.

- *Your company is sinking and you're wondering if it's too late.*

Breathe. This book gives you the tools to evaluate the potential problems so you can answer that question yourself. Startups like Airbnb and Zappos have been on the ropes but bounced back. Maybe that's your current company. Maybe it's because your company isn't ready for growth and you should be focused on product-market fit. How much do your customers actually love your product or service? Is your company focused on the right segment of users? Which marketing channels have you tried and why did you determine that they weren't successful? You'll find the foundation to navigate the world of growth and make the right strategic moves. See chapter 7 where you'll learn what to do when things go wrong.

What other books are out there and how does this one fit in?

There are so many great books and articles out there around this topic. Each one has its own purpose.

To develop your startup idea, check out Paul Graham's Essays (paulgraham.com/startupideas.html).

To test your startup idea, read *Lean Startup* by Eric Ries.

To understand how to track and measure your business, dive into *Lean Analytics* by Alistair Croll and Benjamin Yoskovitz.

To understand all the options for marketing channels, *Traction* by Gabriel Weinberg and Justin Mares is your book.

To learn how to manage your team, read *The Hard Thing About Hard Things* by Ben Horowitz.

To get a history lesson on growth hacking, dive into *Hacking Growth* by Sean Ellis and Morgan Brown.

To get a detailed playbook about growing your startup, you've come to the right place. Keep reading.

When is the right time to read this book?

Before you do anything around growing a company, you'll want to establish a foundation in growth marketing. It's about understanding the basics, analyzing case studies and leaning on a playbook to help you power through your own business growth. Developing this mental model around growth is what will allow you to guide your thought process and it will help solidify your decisions.

It'll help you be more creative in your approach and, most

importantly, it'll help you become confident in your growth ideas and how you'll make them a reality.

Are you testing every possible distribution channel to uncover more users, or are you just seeing how many people like your latest Instagram posts?

Who should NOT read this book?

People who want pages loaded with fluffy marketing content and minimal details. Those looking for a beautifully constructed piece of writing with zero grammatical errors. And Sean Ellis because he invented growth hacking.

CHAPTER 1 CHEAT SHEET

- This is a playbook with actionable steps you can take right now.
- This book is for beginner and proven professionals who want to reset their approach to growth.

2. The Real Reason Startups Fail

> **"Most businesses actually get zero distribution channels to work. Poor distribution—not product—is the number one cause of failure." —Peter Thiel, PayPal cofounder and investor**

Let's go through your thought process as you launch a product:

"I have the best idea ever."

...

I'm so excited I can't sleep. I'm doing it. It's happening."

...

"Wait, why aren't more people using it?"

...

"Why aren't my customers coming back?"

...

"My product sucks."

Has your inner dialogue ever gone down this road?

Well, your product (probably) doesn't suck. Lots of this self-inflicted pain is caused because you're expecting to create the next big thing, but you can't acquire one user other than your mom. You're not seeing instant user growth. People aren't falling in love with your product like you thought they would.

Below is a chart of the top 20 reasons startups fail, according to CB Insights:

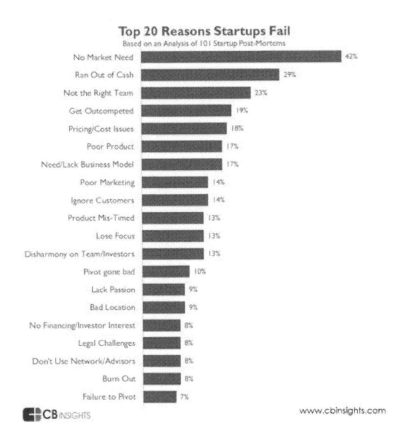

Top 20 Reasons Startups Fail
Based on an Analysis of 101 Startup Post-Mortems

Reason	%
No Market Need	42%
Ran Out of Cash	29%
Not the Right Team	23%
Get Outcompeted	19%
Pricing/Cost Issues	18%
Poor Product	17%
Need/Lack Business Model	17%
Poor Marketing	14%
Ignore Customers	14%
Product Mis-Timed	13%
Lose Focus	13%
Disharmony on Team/Investors	13%
Pivot gone bad	10%
Lack Passion	9%
Bad Location	9%
No Financing/Investor Interest	8%
Legal Challenges	8%
Don't Use Network/Advisors	8%
Burn Out	8%
Failure to Pivot	7%

CB INSIGHTS   www.cbinsights.com

You'll see that 42% of startups failed because there was no market need for that product or service. They either didn't create something that people wanted or they were targeting the wrong users.

"So what?" you say. "If I build a great product, it will sell itself."

Wrong.

The best product doesn't always win. What wins? It's a product that satisfies the right market. Are you putting the same amount of care and attention into your growth strategy as you are into building your actual product?

We'll talk about how to identify whether the problem lies with your product or your distribution plan in chapter 4. Maybe your product is amazing. Maybe you did everything right and your product just needs to be discovered. Maybe your initial idea isn't the right idea, but it's two iterations away from something great.

The problem could be that **you're not connecting your product to potential users the right way.** Your distribution plan isn't thought out and it's taking you down the wrong path. Maybe you're not getting the product in front of the right users or getting the feedback you need. Maybe there is too much friction between your product and your potential customers. Maybe you didn't put enough thought into your user-acquisition strategy or your messaging.

WARNING: Over 60% of your growth experiments will fail. Luckily, you only need one to work.

You could have a ground-breaking iPhone app but you aren't optimized for Apple's App Store. You haven't connected with an app sales rep and you have no idea how to do any paid marketing to get app downloads. Heck, maybe you don't even know how to calculate your customer acquisition cost (CAC) against the lifetime value (LTV) of your customer.

Quick tip: A basic rule of thumb on CAC and LTV is that you want a 3:1 ratio with your LTV being 3x of your CAC. Example: Spend $30 to get $90.

You could have a stunning clothing line for the maternity

category but you have no idea how to optimize your Shopify site for organic traffic. You could be ignoring some of the best keywords like "baby shower dresses" that get a high volume of monthly traffic (it's 50,000 per month, according to Google Keyword Planner).

Maybe you don't understand the true power of affiliate marketing and influencer marketing in e-commerce fashion.

You could be an incredible service for Ruby developers and you never even tried to connect with your potential customers through online forums or online marketing for offline events through Meetup.com.

What does this mean? It means the doubters, the haters and the I-told-you-so-ers are feeling good right now. You're losing hope in your product because you aren't growing.

But the truth is, it might not be the idea or the product. It could be that you aren't using the right framework to uncover your opportunities for growth, the opportunities to put your product in front of the right people at the right time.

If you build it, they will...not give a sh*t

Unless you've invented free money. Users usually don't just magically appear. You need to make sure you understand that. Know that you will launch a product and nothing will change. Yes, you'll get some initial traffic from press, but that goes away.

This comes as a surprise to people. Why is that? Because the overnight success of a startup has been romanticized to a point where it's corrupted how people view growth. It has influenced how people view marketing and it's setting people up to fail. If you aren't thinking about how you're acquiring users, you're going to have some tough days ahead. You need to understand your market and be relentless about connecting with them.

Imagine if BuzzFeed launched as a print publication instead of a social-first online publication on Facebook. What if Groupon hadn't worked so hard to craft an email strategy for its retention marketing plan? What if Mint hadn't used beautifully crafted infographics on its blog to build trust for their personal finance app? What if Dropbox hadn't used free storage as a referral marketing program and kept trying to fine-tune its paid advertisements? What if PayPal hadn't stopped trying to do partnerships with banks to focus on a viral growth strategy to give away money to new users?

For every growth success story there are 10 more stories about the thing that failed before they found their ideal distribution channel. So what does this mean? What is the silver bullet for growth marketing?

The silver bullet is...that there ISN'T a silver bullet.

It's not about tactics and tricks. It's about an approach and process that will help you figure out the best way to align your product with the ideal users. That's what we're going to talk about. It's about how you can ensure success before you even launch a product.

It's about the strategy to sustainable growth. Are you putting the same amount of care and attention into your marketing as you are into building your product?

Jay Baer, a *New York Times* best-selling author and the founder of Convince and Convert, says, "Make your marketing so useful people would pay you for it."

The best growth marketing plans are made up of lots of lead bullets. These one-off growth hacks are not going to make or break the success of a company.

Relentless focus is the multiplier that turns your idea into something valuable. Not just getting lucky, but consistently making your own luck, over and over again. But it's impossible to do this if you don't have a system.

You need a method of deciding on the right combination of marketing channels, data analysis and growth strategy. Define a set of rules for deciding how and when to make changes as you learn more about your business model and the industry in which it operates. Run multiple checks to make sure you're on pace to achieve your goals.

It's worth the effort up front to do a little research to figure out:

- Does my target customer hang out online?
- If so, where?
- How do I get to them?

You can reach moms online. You can reach gamers online. You can certainly reach and sell to marketers online. But can you reach dentists and masonry professionals at scale online?

Some say that distribution can save your startup. Correction: the *right* distribution strategy can save your startup.

The right distribution strategy connects your solution to the people who have the problem in a frictionless way. It forces you to connect the two by finding the right path or paths to uncover the people who will love your product. By focusing on distribution, you're starting with the end in mind. You're setting yourself up for success.

CHAPTER 2 CHEAT SHEET

- Most companies fail because they haven't identified a market for its product.
- The silver bullet to growth marketing is that there isn't a silver bullet. It's about a process for uncovering sustainable growth channels.

- Your target demographic/customers will dictate what marketing channels are an option for your business.

3. Growth Marketing 101

"In real estate, the wisdom says, 'Location, location, location.' In consumer internet, think, 'Distribution, distribution, distribution.'" —Reid Hoffman, LinkedIn founder

Growth marketing, a history lesson.

Marketing is simply a channel that connects your product to your customers.

Originally, it was just word-of-mouth marketing. Then newspapers came into existence, then radio and eventually TV.

These channels got better, but the cost to be on these channels stayed high. It also gave the power to people that owned these channels and the people that could afford these channels.

Yes, I know you already know this, but stay with me.

Then the internet happened and it flipped everything on its head. Chaos ensued.

The number of distribution channels quickly doubled and tripled because of the internet. Channels emerged that were more personal, more relevant, more timely, and, most importantly, cheaper than everything else. We're talking websites, blogs, social media, messaging, email marketing, forums, SMS, etc.

Plus, it wasn't just about content. People who understood how these channels work (looking at the developers, coders and

SEO specialist of the world) were able to maximize these channels for scale and growth. Thanks to the internet, marketing now has a technical component to it.

This shift made the barrier for companies to enter extremely low. Old-school publishers that were industry leaders found themselves losing to younger, smaller and more agile internet platforms. It wasn't about money. It was about rapid innovation.

Online channels like websites, blogs, email newsletters, social networks and messaging platforms emerged as the favorites in the eyes of consumers. They were much more engaging and rich in experience.

The brave brands that latched onto these channels before the masses caught on found themselves beautifully positioned to grow its user base at an insane pace. If they could connect the right platform with the right user, they struck marketing gold. The ones that didn't adapt started to fall farther and farther behind.

Let's talk about a few of those success stories by platform.

Blogs

Have you heard of Bill Simmons, "the BostonSports Guy"? He was the top editor at ESPN and now he is with HBO and the owner of The Ringer website. Before he became a media mogul he was a bartender in Boston with a blog.

He was simply the Boston Sports Guy who went on rants about the Celtics and Red Sox via his AOL account. He wanted to write for traditional media outlets like *The Boston Globe* but he would have had to work for years to get that same audience reach. The key was that he started blogging on this emerging platform as it was gaining momentum and before it became oversaturated.

That, combined with his high-quality product (his writing),

created the perfect formula for his success. New Medium + Quality Product = Rapid growth.

Email

You might not remember this (I'm looking at the millennials out there), but your inbox open rate used to be over 90%. This was before Google sliced your inbox into folders and before you got spammed by a Nigerian prince looking to borrow money. That was a time when companies like Groupon and DailyCandy started to leverage this channel.

DailyCandy was a media company that told influential women in urban areas the most important thing they needed to know each day. They didn't push their website and they didn't launch a print magazine. They focused on crafting the best email newsletter every single day. That's it. They did this very well with emails that were 150 words and targeted by location. Everyone was using email for personal messaging so Daily Candy's content was well positioned to be easily shared and distributed. This meant the Daily Candy brand was reaching a lot of women and at a very low customer acquisition cost. The result: they built up such a significant user base that Comcast acquired them for $150 million.

Social Media

With social media, we saw companies like BuzzFeed and Upworthy build content specifically for this platform. On Instagram, influencers like Josh Ostrovsky, aka, "@thefatjewish," started as a silly account that posted funny GIFs and photos. But he joined Instagram at the perfect moment. It was outpacing Facebook's growth rate and it wasn't oversaturated yet. His sharable content plus the platform's ridiculous growth rate resulted in him getting over 7 million users in one year. He built an audience on Instagram and then took it to YouTube with his online TV channel. He even took it to the liquor stores with his own rosé called, White Girl Rosé.

App Store

When Evernote launched their mobile app they did it right as the Apple App Store was starting to take off. Their app got featured on the front page of the App Store and the result was thousands of downloads within one day. Apple users were early adopters of new technology, so they were open to using this new app called Evernote. After that first launch, Evernote decided to always time their new product launches with any new iPhone or Apple product release. They saw the Apple app store as this new distribution channel. Their founder Phil Libin said, "We really killed ourselves in the first couple of years to always be in all of the app store launches on day one." Their hard work paid off and they averaged 19,000 new sign-ups per day.

The common theme is the following:

Right Product + Right Channel + Right Time = Accelerated Growth

Below is a chart created by Silicon Valley entrepreneur and investor James Currier and updated by Growth Tribe cofounder Peter Van Sabben, showing different marketing distribution channels based on their timing and their effectiveness.

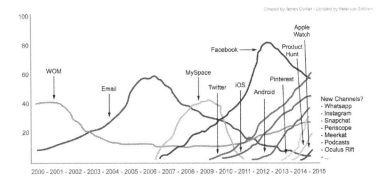

Unfortunately, this is much easier said than done.

What if you can't time the right distribution channel at the right time? What if your product isn't naturally shareable or viral? Sorry, insurance companies and personal finance apps.

What if the best channel for you is oversaturated? What if you can't wait for the next Instagram because you're running out of money?

I hear you.

We're going to take a step back and talk about how to approach growth in a constantly changing environment, how to utilize the existing channels and how to find the right channel for your customers. We will dive into the different philosophies around growth marketing.

But first, let's talk about the end game: Finding a sustainable growth channel. We'll determine the difference between good growth and bad growth.

The Goal Isn't Just Growth. It's GOOD Growth

What does growth really mean? What is the right growth and

what is the wrong growth? Bad growth is when you use a tactic that results in getting people to your site and they don't take the action you want and never come back. (For example, they don't join, they don't make a purchase or they don't engage with your content.) It's easy to be fooled by "bad growth."

Imagine that you have a lot of money to spend on paid marketing channels like Facebook and Google AdWords—thanks, investors! You could optimize your ads to send more and more people to your site each month. This would result in a nice line graph that shows your sessions growth going up and to the right. This might make you feel smart and your partners will feel good. And your investors might think you're brilliant.

But a deeper look into the data would show some ugly truths. Vanity metrics (like page views) could be going up, but your percentage of repeat users might be decreasing. Your churn rates could rise. Your retention rate might be horrible. The lifetime value of your user could be so low that it doesn't justify the amount of money you're dumping into ads. It would just be a matter of time before your amazing growth rate was exposed for what it really is.

Below is a graph from Alex Schultz, vice president of growth at Facebook, that outlines what good growth and bad growth look like. Good growth means retention is strong and users come back—it's the line that flattens out. Bad growth is when users come once and then never come back again—it's the line that face-plants into the x-axis. Ouch.

Retention

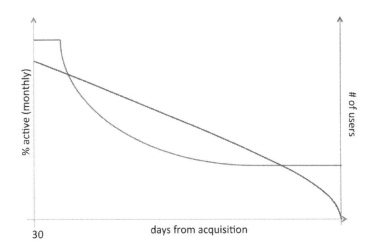

So what is good growth?

Good growth is growth that is sustainable for your business model. It's free channels that help you acquire quality customers that need your product or service. It's paid channels with a positive net return. You're getting more money out of the users than it cost to acquire them. Your CAC (customer acquisition cost) is less than the LTV (lifetime value of a customer).

That also means your retention curve doesn't dive into the ground. It flattens out over time because you have users that are returning to your site.

It's good growth that brings users to the site and has them taking the action that you want, like signing up for your email list, creating an account, interacting with users, making a purchase or inviting friends to your website.

It's growth experiments that aren't one-time hacks. They are repeatable and scalable.

Get it? Got it? Good!

Now that you understand the difference between good growth and bad growth let's look at the existing frameworks that already exist around growth. We're going to do a brief summary on the following four frameworks, but I highly recommend reading more about them from their respective books to truly do them justice.

The ICE Score by Sean Ellis

Sean Ellis, former head of growth at Dropbox, came up with the phrase "growth hacker" in 2010 when he was trying to hire his replacement. The marketing candidates weren't working out because he wanted marketers that were more data and product driven. We'll get into this in more detail in chapter 8.

In addition to being the growth hacker pioneer, he also developed the ICE score framework to allow teams to easily prioritize their growth experiments. This method allows you to list out all of your growth ideas and score each one by three categories: impact, confidence and ease.

Then you focus on two to five experiments per week based on which ones have the highest score. This framework allows you to quantify each experiment idea so you can use data to drive what experiment you should focus on.

As an example, you could list the growth marketing idea of launching dynamic product ads on Facebook for your e-commerce store. This might get a 7 for impact, a 9 for confidence and an 8 for ease. The impact is high because it's hitting a very engaged user, and your confidence is also strong because you have had good success with your paid campaigns on Facebook.

You also rank the ease of 8 because your e-commerce store is on Shopify and they have a seamless integration with Facebook. It just requires you checking the connection and reviewing the dynamic product catalog.

Below is an example of the ICE framework used by the growthhackers.com software. It allows you to prioritize your growth experiments based on impact, confidence and ease of implementation. (Image is from Anna Rehermann.)

Lean Startup by Eric Ries

The *Lean Startup* by Eric Ries has become so famous that it has warranted spin-off books, conferences and podcasts. It's an inspiring read about getting to product-market fit by talking to your customers.

In his book, Eric talks about how to grow after you have product-market fit. He says there are three engines that drive growth for a startup. The sticky engine, the virality engine and the paid engine. Below is a breakdown of his framework and what each engine means for that business.

1. *Sticky Engine:* Focus on getting your customers and users to come back to your platform and use your product. Eric believes that engagement and retention are a great (or maybe even the best) predictor of success.
2. *Virality Engine:* Focus on existing users spreading the word about your product or service. The measurement for this is viral coefficient. It's the number of new users that each existing user brings to the product.
3. *Paid Engine:* Focus on getting payment from your users and monetizing your product. It's the final metric that determines if you have a sustainable business model. Getting paid allows you to funnel that money back into the business to spend on acquisition and other growth channels.

Pirate Metrics by Dave McClure

Dave McClure is an entrepreneur, a venture capitalist, and founder of the startup accelerator called *500 Startups*. He created the Pirate Metrics framework to breakdown the five key components of growing a successful company.

The name comes from the acronym for the metrics that a startup must focus on—acquisition, activation, retention, revenue and referral—or AARRR. This is something that my growth teams think about every week when trying to decide what to focus on at that moment. (Image below is from startitup.com.)

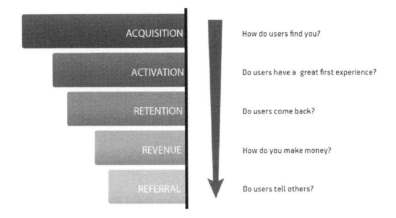

ACQUISITION	How do users find you?
ACTIVATION	Do users have a great first experience?
RETENTION	Do users come back?
REVENUE	How do you make money?
REFERRAL	Do users tell others?

This framework flows as a conversion funnel for the customer or user. Here's how you can look at each part of the funnel and how it relates to your business:

- *Acquisition:* How do you get users to your website? This could include growth ideas like SEO, SEM, email, PR, content marketing, social media, ads, etc.
- *Activation:* How do you get visitors to take action on your website? This could mean sign-ups, creating a profile, submitting content, etc.
- *Retention:* How do you get users to return to your platform? This could include email marketing, push notifications, social media, updates, etc.
- *Revenue:* How do you get paid from a user's activity? Ways to make money include transactions, subscriptions, affiliate fees, clicks, etc.
- *Referral:* How are users promoting your product to their network? Referral mechanisms include emails, texts, social media, plug-ins, widgets, etc.

The Bullseye Framework by Gabriel Weinberg

Gabriel Weinberg is the founder of the privacy-protecting search engine DuckDuckGo and the coauthor of *Traction*, a book that breaks down the 19 channels for getting traction with users. I recommend reading this book for the case studies alone.

He came up with the bullseye framework in his book on how to navigate all the options to find the right one for you. Gabriel says it's a five-step process to find your channels for testing: brainstorm, rank, prioritize, test, and focus on what works. You're aiming for the "bullseye"—the one traction channel that will unlock your next growth stage.

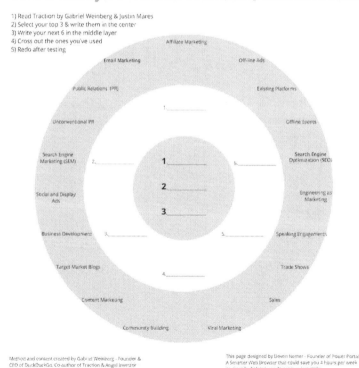

The Bullseye Framework For finding the best traction channels

1) Read Traction by Gabriel Weinberg & Justin Mares
2) Select your top 3 & write them in the center
3) Write your next 6 in the middle layer
4) Cross out the ones you've used
5) Redo after testing

Method and content created by Gabriel Weinberg - Founder & CEO of DuckDuckGo, Co-author of Traction & Angel Investor

This page designed by Deven Nemer - Founder of Power Portal A Smarter Web Browser that could save you 4 hours per week or more by helping you do more in less clicks

How the bullseye framework works:

- *Brainstorm:* Come up with reasonable ways you might use each of the 19 traction channels.
- *Rank:* Place each of the traction channels into one of three columns, with each column representing a concentric circle in the bullseye: Column A (Inner Circle): which traction channels seem most promising right now? Column B (Potential): which traction channels seem like they could possibly work? Column C (Long-shot): which traction channels seem like long-shots?
- *Prioritize:* Identify your inner circle by selecting three traction channels that seem most promising.
- *Test:* Put your ideas into the real world. The goal of this step is to find out which of the traction channels in your inner circle are worth focusing on.
- *Focus on What Works:* One of the traction channels you tested in your inner circle will produce promising results. That's when you start directing your traction efforts and resources toward that most promising channel. One traction channel dominates in terms of customer acquisition.

Growth Loops by Brian Balfour

Brian Balfour is the founder of Reforge, a growth program for experienced practitioners, and he created the Growth Loops process. Brian says the following about growth loops on reforge.com:

"The fastest growing products are better represented as a system of loops, not funnels. Loops are closed systems where the inputs through some process generates more of an output that can be reinvested in the input. There are growth loops that serve different value creation including new users, returning users, defensibility, or efficiency." (Image below is from reforge.com.)

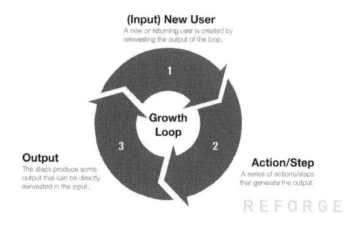

What Can We Learn from These Frameworks?

All of these frameworks are powerful when used the right way. There are some overlaps with each of them, but the key takeaways are that: (1) you should only market a product worthy of your marketing; and (2) once you do, it's about testing and iterating on the growth experiments that can have the biggest impact.

But always remember that you should only start marketing if you have something that customers actually want. Do you have product-market fit? If not, stop marketing and get to product-market fit.

The FACT Framework for Growth by Jim Huffman (me)

After advising various startups and fortune 500 companies, I have developed a preference for different frameworks and processes. For managing a team, I like a combination of the bullseye framework and the ICE process, and we'll talk about how to manage your process in chapter 8.

This framework isn't about running a team or a process. This is about the strategy for developing your growth marketing plan. Basically, where to start on day one.

The key component of the FACT framework is to design your strategy around one thing: your customer. The better you understand your customer the better you'll be as a growth marketer. Here's a breakdown of the FACT framework:

- **F**ind your customers
- **A**cquire your customers
- **C**onvert your customers
- **T**urn your customers into marketers

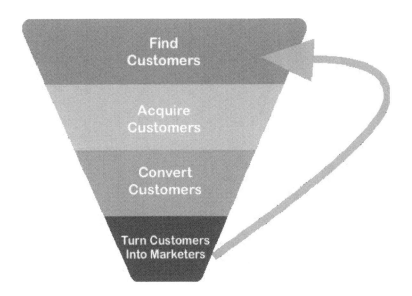

- *Find your customers*

In chapter 5, we will talk about how to uncover where your customers live online. This could be the forums they frequent on Reddit or the influencers that they follow on Instagram. From analyzing competitors to building out user personas, we will pin-point where these people live online and the right way to get in front of them. With one exercise, you will actually find 1,000,000 potential customers online. Side note: if you can't find one million potential customers online then you better be selling something with a high price point.

- *Acquire your customers*

After you have identified where your customers live online, the next questions is, how can you make the right first impression? What's the right way to get in front of them and what is the right messaging? It could be through direct outreach from the founder or through a paid channel with the right editorial touch. It could also be through offline meetups and online referrals.

Regarding the message, you want to speak their language and address the common pain-points in their industry. Remember, if you try to be everything to everyone then you will disappoint everyone. Think of your product as an exclusive club that is only open for a specific type of person. We'll get into lots of options for acquisition in chapter 8.

- *Convert your customers*

You have identified your ideal customer and you have determined the right channel for acquiring these customers.

Next, you need to make sure you can convert them into a loyal customer.

How do you turn visitors into subscribers, customers or users? How are you bringing customers back to your site and how long before their next interaction or transaction? Conversion and retention will make or break companies. We'll dive into the best practices for converting and retaining customers in chapter 6 and chapter 8.

- *Turn your customers into marketers*

Once you've activated your customer, the next goal is turning that customer into a marketer. Let me pause and say one thing: this is the most powerful thing you can do in online marketing. This means building a user experience that turns a first time customer into a brand advocate (online or offline) that helps you get new customers for free.

This could be sharing your website URL with their friends via a social channel or getting them to actually invite people to use your product through email. We'll go through the best practices for doing this at the end of chapter 8 when we talk about scaling tactics with growth marketing and growth hackers.

The main goal with the FACT Framework is to always put the customer first in every step you take and every part of the funnel. From how to identify them online to how to give them a reason to want to convert, marketing is about adding value for your customer, so I want that to come through in this framework. The rest of this book feeds into this four-step strategy.

In the next chapter, we're going to talk about how to know if you are ready for growth. And most importantly, how to use product-market fit to drive your entire growth strategy.

CHAPTER 3 CHEAT SHEET

- The internet has created a marketing landscape that favors companies that are both fast and technical.
- There are many existing growth frameworks to choose from. They include Sean Ellis's ICE framework, Dave McClure's Pirate Metrics, Eric Reis's *The Lean Startup* and Gabriel Weinberg's Bullseye framework.
- The FACT Framework allows you to build your strategy around your customer and their interactions with your brand.
- Start with the customer's digital footprint and end with the goal of turning that customer into a marketer.

4. How to Know You're Ready for Growth

"You want some good marketing advice, make stuff that people want." —Paul Graham, Founder of Y Combinator

The secret to growth marketing happens before you do any marketing.

It happens when you pick a phenomenal product or service that's worthy of your time and energy.

A great product will make you look like a brilliant marketer. It will allow you to roll out experiments and determine if a distribution channel works or doesn't work very quickly.

A great product will make you excited to focus on growth.

A great product will market itself—you just have to find the right marketing avenue to send it down.

Put another way, only invest in growth once you have product-market fit. If you don't have product-market fit then you should not be focused on growth. You need to be focused on your customers and figuring out how to make a product or service that they truly need.

You shouldn't need *any* marketing to find 10 target customers to try your product. Listen to their feedback and iterate. Until you can convince a handful of them to shout, "Shut up and take my money!" don't focus on growth. You don't have product-market fit.

Wait, what is product-market fit?

According to venture capitalist Marc Andreessen, this is the definition of product-market fit:

"Product-market fit means being in a good market with a product that can satisfy that market.

You can always feel when product/market fit isn't happening. The customers aren't quite getting value out of the product, word of mouth isn't spreading, usage isn't growing that fast, press reviews are kind of "blah," the sales cycle takes too long, and lots of deals never close.

And you can always feel product-market fit when it's happening. The customers are buying the product just as fast as you can make it—or usage is growing just as fast as you can add more servers. Money from customers is piling up in your company checking account. You're hiring sales and customer support staff as fast as you can. Reporters are calling because they've heard about your hot new thing and they want to talk to you about it. You start getting entrepreneur of the year awards from Harvard Business School. Investment bankers are staking out your house. You could eat free for a year at Buck's."

Simply put, you'll know it when you have it because you cannot handle the demand.

Product-market fit happens when you are painfully better than any alternative out there. That could be a competitor or a previous way of life. For example: hailing an Uber on your phone from a restaurant was significantly better than standing in the rain with your hand in the air looking for a cab.

Are you 10 times better than the next best option?

Getting to product-market fit starts with solving a problem. It's finding a pain point and getting rid of it. It's solving that problem in a way that is 10 times better than the next best alternative. Yes, you could solve a problem but if it's only two times better than the industry leader then it's not going to be that noteworthy. In most cases, if won't be great enough to switch from what they're doing to get people to tell their friends about it.

Sometimes it might not be about being better than a competitor. Your competition might not be an actual company. Your real competition could be unimportance or indifference. Your product or service could solve a problem, but if people don't care, the problem might not be that important. It might not be a true pain and they don't care about what you built.

For bootstrapped founders trying to make $10,000/month in MRR (monthly recurring revenue), you might approach it from a conflicting perspective. You don't have to invent anything new or something that's necessarily 10X better than everyone. You can build something slightly above average, have a great growth plan, and still crush your goals. The key thing is that you put your own spin on a tried-and-true idea that targets a very specific user.

Rob Sobers lays out this approach in his blog post titled, "Easy Mode" (https://robsobers.com/easy-mode/). Here are a few options for product ideas in the B2B space:

- **The Lightweight Product.** Fewer features, but much better UX (Drip, Buffer)
- **The Delightful Product.** Give your product a personality and focus on the little details that make people smile (Freckle, Slack)
- **The Single-Purpose Product.** Do one thing exceptionally well with zero distractions (Pinboard, TinyLetter)
- **The Opinionated Product.** Take a strong stance on *how* a problem should be solved (e.g., budgeting

software YNAB forces you to manually enter expenses so you're conscious of your spending)

Is it a vitamin or aspirin?

If it's solving a real pain, people will be happy to use it regardless of the flaws it may have in the early days. Users will be shouting to you that they love it and they'll give ideas on what they want you to do to make it better. If it's a vitamin people will say "oh, that's cool I would totally use that," and then time passes and they don't use your product. If it's not a solution they're actively searching for then they might not use it.

You don't want to create a "nice to have" product. In tough times, the "nice to have" products get thrown out. You want a "must have" product that users can't live without. How do you know if you have a must-have product? Here are a couple of ways to determine if you have product-market fit:

The 40% test

Sean Ellis, former head of growth at Dropbox, says you can determine if you have product-market fit by asking your users just one question: How would they feel if your product went away? You can email them through a free survey tool like SurveyMonkey or Google Forms. If over 40% of your users would be "very disappointed" if your product went away, then you're on to something. Here's how he recommends framing the question:

How would you feel if you could no longer use Buffer's Power scheduler (picture above)?

Choices	Percentage		Count
Very disappointed		78.26%	36
Somewhat disappointed		19.57%	9
N/A – I don't use Buffer's new power scheduler	2.17%		1
		Total	46

Image from cobloom.com

Do you have "word of mouth" marketing?

"'Tweet' and 'like' buttons isn't word of mouth. Rather, word of mouth comes from content, thoughtfulness, solved problems, and ease of use—in short, the whole experience of a product or service." – *Sean Ellis*

Word-of-mouth marketing is hands down the best marketing a company can get. But how do you measure that? Are people sharing your product? Are they referring friends? Are they talking about your product online or offline? This is usually pretty clear. One way to do that is by calculating your Net Promoter Score (NPS).

NPS is a tool to gauge the loyalty of a brand's customer relationships. The Net Promoter Score is calculated as the difference between the percentage of Promoters and Detractors. The NPS is an absolute number lying between -100 and +100. For instance, if you have 45% Promoters, 35% Passives and 20% Detractors, the NPS will be +25.

If you don't have product-market fit, then you should really be focused on talking to customers and getting feedback on why they don't like your product. The Lean Startup Canvas methodology is a great resource for going down that road.

If you have product-market fit then something amazing will happen. Complete strangers will do free marketing for you. They'll talk about your product at happy hours, at coffee shops and they'll even email you to say how amazing you are.

This is word-of-mouth marketing and it's the best possible marketing channel. It's free and these people will do it with a smile on their face. Sign me up.

Listen to your promoters

When people are talking about your product, you need to do one thing: listen.

What are these enthusiastic promoters saying about your company? What are their exact keywords? Is your product saving them time, money or is it raising their status? Why do they love it? How do they feel after they use your product?

It's so important to understand the language and verbiage that your customers use when talking about your product. Why? Because it's those words that will help shape how you, as a marketer, should be promoting this product. It can drive the copy you use in your ads and on the landing page of your website. You need to use the language of the customer to attract other customers.

Here are examples of how customers simply explain products they love:

Allbirds: "Running shoes made of wool."

Drip: "An email marketing tool designed for drip campaigns."

Snapchat: "Send a text to a friend and then it disappears."

Warby Parker: "Premium glasses for $99."

Universal Standard: "Replace your clothes if you go up or down a size."

Uber: "Tap your phone and a car shows up in five minutes."

Shazam: "An app that tells you who's singing any song."

iPod: "1,000 songs in your pocket"

GrubHub: "Food from any restaurant, delivered to your door."

Hotel Tonight: "Book premium hotels the night of at a discount."

Airbnb: "Turn your spare bedroom into a hotel room."

How easy is it for people to explain your product or service to a friend? Can they convey your value proposition to a group of people at a crowded bar . . . after a few cocktails?

Also, how are people positioning your company against competitors? It's important to know what you are and what you are not. One thing to watch out for is when a competitor emerges in your space with a comparable must-have product. How do your users compare you to them? Positioning is very important if you're in a crowded space.

But what if I don't have customers yet?

You want to start talking to people about your product as soon as possible to get their feedback. Eric Reis goes into this in great detail in the book *The Lean Startup*.

One way to fine-tune your value proposition is with the "mom test." Pitch the company to someone who is removed from the product development process. Yes, you can use your mom. Now, have them pitch the company back to you. How did they do? What keywords did they use? What feature do they focus on? The startups that get real traction are the ones that succeed in this startup version of telephone.

Not ready to tell people about your idea? Struggling with your pitch? Use the following elevator pitch formula to break down why your product or service is special and different. This structure is great for helping you take a step back and understand how to position your company.

For (target customer)
Who (statement of need or opportunity)
(Product name) **is a** (product category)
That (statement of key benefit)

Unlike (competing alternative)
(Product name) (statement of primary differentiation).

Here's an example of the elevator pitch in action for the online women's clothing company, Universal Standard.

For women of any size
Who are looking for elevated looks for their wardrobe
Universal Standard **is a** premium size-inclusive brand
That sells direct to consumers, offering the highest-quality products at the best price.
Unlike plus-size fashion lines, Universal Standard will replace your clothes if your size goes up or down within a year.

Speak their language

As you get feedback from press, customers, friends or even your mom, stockpile all the blurbs that capture the essence of your product in their words. What problem does your product solve? How does it make them feel? What is their favorite feature? How does it benefit them? Take all of their feedback and put it into one sheet. This is the starting point for your marketing messaging.

As an example, BeOn, a caffeinated chocolate snack, started to get testimonials from customers on why they loved the product. Customers kept saying the energy gems provided a hit of energy without the crash one gets from coffee or energy drinks. After seeing this pattern, BeOn started adding this benefit of "no crash" into its marketing campaigns.

When it comes to messaging, you're limited in the attention a person will give your brand. That means you need to: (1) give them a message that will resonate; and (2) give it to them in their own language. This message should be consistent no matter where they see it: your homepage, your About Us page, your social channels, your blog, your welcome email, your messaging tool—anyplace where you would touch a potential user. But it starts with your homepage. In chapter 8 about activation, we'll break down how to lay out the perfect home page.

CHAPTER 4 CHEAT SHEET

- Product-Market Fit First: Don't focus on growth marketing until you know you have product-market fit.
- Surveys: Leverage Sean Ellis's 40% test or NPS surveys to quantify if you have product-market fit.
- Speak Their Language: Leverage the language of your top customers or brand ambassadors for your marketing and product copy.

5. PLAYBOOK: How to Uncover Your Growth Opportunities

"Many entrepreneurs who build great products simply don't have a good distribution strategy. Even worse is when they insist that they don't need one, or call no distribution strategy a 'viral marketing strategy' ... a16z is a sucker for people who have sales and marketing figured out." —Marc Andreessen, Venture Capitalist at a16z

Congrats, you have product-market fit.

Now it's time to tell your market about your product. It's time to develop a growth strategy.

This is like building a house.

You want to have a blueprint first and then get started on building. It's the same thing for growth. After you have product-market fit, you want to develop the right growth plan to scale the right way.

It's easy to want to do some of the things you hear people talking about on podcasts or in articles you read on TechCrunch. Things like paid acquisition ("time to do Facebook ads") or conferences ("I'm going to speak on panels") can be very appetizing.

I'm not saying you shouldn't do those things, but you should make sure you've done your research first. You need to be confident that you're focusing on the right channels for your specific audience.

Your user-acquisition strategy may not be the same as other companies in other industries. Hey, it might not even be the same as your direct competitor's. This section will help you uncover what the right distribution channels are for finding potential customers.

It's amazing to me how much time and money can go into a marketing plan without even thinking through the customer mindset or the customer persona. We will go over what to factor in when you're building your growth strategy.

Your end goal will be to optimize every phase of that funnel. As a reminder, here is the FACT Framework funnel:

- **F**ind your customers
- **A**cquire your customers
- **C**onvert your customers
- **T**urn your customers into marketers

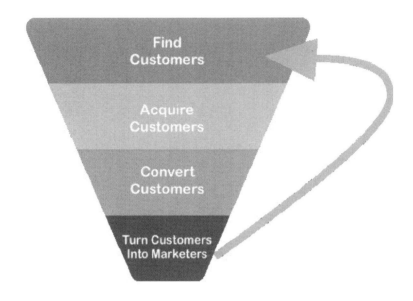

Before running experiments and trying to grow, it's important to understand your entire marketing landscape. It's time to do the homework to uncover any growth opportunities. You're about to learn how to understand the following:

- Competitive landscape
- Industry landscape
- Customer landscape

How to Understand Your Competitors

Competitive Analysis: Give Yourself a Head Start

By focusing on your competitors, you'll start to understand their marketing priorities and positioning within the market. It also shows you where they are and, more importantly, where they are not.

It allows you to see what's working in your industry and what's not. You can understand how they are positioned within your market and what makes them unique.

Understand a Competitor's Traffic

First, you want to understand where their traffic is coming from. By using a "marketing intelligence" tool such as SimilarWeb, you can see the number of visits they're getting per month and where those visits are coming from. It'll be broken down into organic traffic (from search engines such as Google and Bing), direct traffic (users going direct to the company URL), referral traffic (users coming from other websites like TechCrunch, Business Insider, etc.) and social traffic (users coming from social networks).

If you see that your competitors are getting over 30% of traffic from search then you'll want to dive in and understand their technical SEO structure on their site and the top keywords they're ranking for on Google and various search engines. What keywords are paid keywords and what keywords are organic? Translation: what search terms are they paying for and what search terms are they getting for free?

Tools like SEMrush and Moz allow you to dive into their organic traffic profile even more. They also allow you to see the top backlinks your competitors are getting. Meaning: the websites have sent them the most traffic. This way you can see if it's better to go after niche blogs or wide-ranging publications.

Understand a Competitor's Brand Position

To understand their brand positioning, go to the homepage of every competitor and write down the main headline and the first call to action on the site. How do they position themselves and what do they ask users to do? Are they more benefit-focused and talk about the user or do they hype up a new technology they created? Who are they speaking to and how are they talking to them? What language are they using—conversational terms or technical speak?

Analyze the Main Call to Action

Are they trying to get people to start a free trial or are they optimizing to get people to download an ebook?
Do they offer a free trial or 20% for buying their product?
Do they give out a checklist or guide to educate the potential customer about the product?
Look at all of your competitors and put them side by side to understand common themes and opportunities with positioning.

For a deeper look at their ongoing marketing strategy, you want to get a sample of email newsletters and ads from each competitor. You can do this with a simple hack: join their email newsletter and watch the onboarding campaigns and newsletters come in. You can also use a tool like MailCharts to look at every email campaign a company sends and understand how often they send newsletters. MailCharts is a paid service, but worth it if you want to dive deep into the email analysis.

Pay attention to the following when analyzing your competitors' emails:

- Frequency of send (once per week or once per day)
- The "from" name they use. Is it from the company or from the founder?
- How segmented or personalized is the content? Are they targeting you based on certain characteristics?
- What products are they pushing in the first few weeks?
- Do the emails contain only text or are there pretty graphics and GIFs?

For access to your competitors' ads, visit their website and put something in your cart. Then you'll start to be retargeted with ads on Facebook and sites that are on their remarketing network. You'll be able to see how they try to pull you back to their site. For a bigger sample size of ads from your competition, check out Adbeat to see their top-performing ad campaigns.

Summary

With these tools, you can recreate almost the entire marketing funnel for a company to understand that brand's marketing strategy. Put these strategies side by side and ask yourself how can you make an experience that's better than this? Or how can you innovate on some of these tactics? For an example on how to build this analysis, go to growthmarketersplaybook.com and download the growth templates to make your own.

How to Understand Your Industry

Before you enter any industry you need to ask yourself "What are the common pain points in this industry?" Unless you're creating your own category or business model, you'll find that the common issues are very well known.

Below is a chart from Ben Yoskovitz that highlights the common pain points by industry.

INDUSTRY	PAIN POINT
e-Commerce	CAC (customer acquisition cost) vs. LTV (lifetime value)—margins are usually very small. A $10M e-commerce business is small.
SaaS (Software as a Service)	Freemium requires tens of millions of free users. They can be expensive to support. Will enough convert?
Mobile Apps	The average number of apps downloaded by North Americans is down. Monetizing is incredibly hard. Popularity is fleeting.
Marketplace	Chicken and egg problem. Supply and demand. How do you build up both sides of the market enough?
Media	Real monetization requires hundreds of millions of engaged visitors. People's attention is hard to capture and keep.
UGC (User-Generated Content Sites)	Content creation. Will it be enough? Will enough people do it? Why?

For e-commerce companies, the main issue always comes back to how much it costs to acquire a customer. What's your CAC (customer acquisition cost) vs. how much a user will spend with you over their LTV (lifetime value)? If it costs $100 to acquire a customer, but they spend $1,000 per year, those numbers work.

But if you're spending $20 to get a user and they never spend more than $15, those numbers don't support a sustainable business model.

If you're a SaaS (software as a service) business with a freemium model, factor in how many users you need to acquire because only a small percentage of those users will actually convert to paid users. Plus, how long will it take to get a user to convert?

Within your industry, what type of business model do you have? Below is a graphic from *Lean Analytics* that showcases the three types of business models for an e-commerce company.

Metrics help you know yourself:

Customers that buy >1x in 90d	Then you are in this mode	Your customers will buy from you	You are just like	Focus on
1-15%	Acquisition	Once	70% of retailers	Low cost of acquisition, high checkout
15-30%	Hybrid	2-2.5 per year	20% of retailers	Increasing return rate, market share
>30%	Loyalty	>2.5 per year	10% of retailers	Loyalty, selection, inventory size

If you only sell your product once per year to one customer, then your marketing efforts are more focused around a low CAC (customer acquisition cost) and upselling at checkout. Examples of these businesses include Christmas trees, diamond rings and vacation packages. Why do you think every jeweler also offers ring insurance and beautiful custom boxes? They're trying to increase your lifetime value because they might not ever see you again.

If you're an e-commerce company that sells to a customer more than 2.5 times per year, then you care more about customer service, customer loyalty and offering a wide selection of options. Examples include diaper companies, grocery stores and clothing retailers. It's not about maximizing a one-time spend but optimizing for satisfaction so a customer comes back again and again.

Summary

Based on your industry or your business model, you should have an idea on the big hurdles you'll need to leap as a marketer. Those pain points can end up being your opportunities if you approach them the right way.

How to Understand Your Customers

Knowing your business model, your competitors and your industry is very important, but there is nothing more important than truly understanding your customers.

Taking the time to do this can't be overstated. Here's a process and some tools that can help you in this area:

Step 1: Understand the Interests of Potential Customers

In its simplest form, marketing is about connecting your product or service with actual people. Who are these people? Where do they live online? Are they in Facebook groups or subreddits? Are they on platforms like Snapchat or Quora? Do they use certain digital products or hardware devices?

A starting point is looking at the customers of your competitors by leveraging the data from the competitive analysis you performed earlier. You know the backlinks that drove traffic to their site, the keywords they used, the social networks they're on and the language that attracts them. Use that information to find these people online and understand their digital footprint.

Here's how you would do that if your company is a men's clothing brand trying to compete with Bonobos. After researching Bonobos.com on Similarweb.com, you'll discover that they get a lot of traffic from Reddit, Cool Hunting, Business Insider and *The Wall Street Journal*. Also, they're aggressive about owning the search phrase "mens pants." Last, the data shows that these visitors look for products at Brooks Brothers, another competitor to inspect.

This research quickly helps us know that one user group is very business minded and they're hitting the Bonobos pants page between articles on *WSJ* and Business Insider. This information can help drive how you target these users, by utilizing promotions around business attire or lookbooks that take place in an urban financial setting.

Next, you'll dig into Reddit because the data shows that Bonobos users live here. After going to Reddit and seeing the conversations around Bonobos, you'll discover that these users love getting into the details of a product and really testing the quality and durability.

This could inspire the idea of pushing a video series to the Reddit community around how you make each product. Just by understanding your customer, it quickly opens up your ideas for marketing toward users similar to the users your competitors have.

Step 2: Build a User Persona Matrix

Next, you'll want to take the information you have on your customers (or soon-to-be customers) and build out user personas. The user personas allow you to put more color around the customers you want to target.

It helps you understand how your ideal users act and think. You need this information so you know how to message a user the right way. Below is how to break down your customer personas:

	Persona
	Fashionable Finance Man
Gender	Male
Age	25–45
Region	Cities
Academic Profile	College Educated
Career	Real Estate, Finance, Management Consulting, Accounting, Lawyer
Marital Status	Single
Family	No kids
Hobbies/ Interest	Running, Skiing, Golf, Football
Income	Over $75,000
Brands they Like	Venmo, Mint, Evernote, Uber, Spotify, Business Insider, WSJ, AMEX, etc.

Give each user persona a headline or tagline. For example: if you're making men's clothing based on the above data then we could start with two groups: One is the "Fashionable Finance Man" and the second is the "Cares About Quality Consumer."

The Fashionable Finance Man is the one that reads the *WSJ* and Business Insider. He lives in a big city, works in finance and cares about style over price because he is also looking at Brooks Brothers.

The "Cares About Quality Consumer" is the professional that works in a creative field and loves using Reddit for product reviews. He cares about the materials of the product and the utility of the clothes. He might work in a big city or remotely and loves the clothes for casual and recreational purposes.

Step 3: Create Your Target List Model

Now that you have created your user personas, let's figure out where these users live online. It's time to build out a model to quantify exactly where each group of users hangout on the internet. We'll do the exercise of creating a bottom-up model showing your target list and actually identifying one million people who would potentially use your product or service.

Yes, create a spreadsheet and list the exact forum, Meetup group, Facebook page, Quora category, Reddit, influencer, organization or website these people frequent. Then put the exact number based on how many people are in that group, how many people follow an influencer or blogger, etc. Then you know exactly where your customers live online. Noah Kagan (CEO of Sumo) calls this quant-based marketing. We call it our customer target list.

Whatever you call it, keep it really simple. It can be an Excel spreadsheet (or a Google sheet) that has the following structure: Row 1: Name of the group/site; Row 2: Number of people in that group; Row 3: The website's URL. The goal is to build this pipeline until you hit over one million potential users.

Here are some ideas for how to find these people:

- Facebook groups related to your industry
- Reddit communities related to your product
- LinkedIn groups in your industry
- Quora discussions around the problem you're solving with your product or service
- Use Buzzsumo to find the most shared content on the web related to your subject
- Use Followerwonk to find the top influencers on Twitter
- Leverage the user data from your competitive analysis (top backlinks and traffic sources)
- Google searches around keywords in your category
- Bloggers and editors in your space

- List of blogs or websites they also follow
- List of organizations and groups they're involved with

For example, the "Cares about Quality Consumer" might follow the blogger A Continuous Lean (ACL) on Instagram. ACL has 60,000 followers on his Instagram feed. Assuming that 70% are male, that's 42,000 potential customers. There's one entry on your customer target list.

Next, go to Reddit and find a men's fashion forum that has 120,000 followers. Congrats, you've found 162,000 potential customers. Now, keep doing this until you hit one million.

To help do this yourself, I created a template for building your own target customer list. **(You can download this exact spreadsheet and all my growth templates at** growthmarketersplaybook.com.)

Why is it important to understand your persona and why is it important to find these people? It helps you understand the customer. But more importantly, it's to show you that these people exist and you know exactly where they are online. By seeing these people online, you'll start to understand them even more so you can build a pipeline of growth experiments targeted toward them.

Here's an example of how Seamless, the online food-ordering service, took its user-persona data and turned it into a partnership strategy that drove significant growth.

Seamless provides food delivery for almost every restaurant in major cities like NYC. After its launch in New York City, Seamless started to get customer data and uncovered that young males were using the product the most frequently. These users were mostly ordering from smartphones and their orders were being sent to their office and not their home.

Seamless figured out that its top user persona was a young single male who was working long hours at investment banks and consulting firms. This insight drove their focus on partnership deals with the top consulting firms and investment banks in Manhattan, like Boston Consulting Group and Goldman Sachs. Pretty smart, huh? They attribute this segment as the key to their initial success.

Now that you've identified these people, it's time to start hitting them up, right? Wrong. You need to take a serious look at your site and make sure you're prepared to activate these users. We're talking conversion rate optimization (CRO), marketing infrastructure and analytics. That's what we'll talk about in the next chapter.

Chapter 5 Cheat Sheet

- Understand what's working for your competitors to understand which marketing channels you want to try or stay away from.
- What are the common pain points of your industry and how can you overcome them with your marketing strategy.
- Develop your customer personas to truly understand your end user and where they live online.
- Build a target customer list of one million users.

6. PLAYBOOK: How to Set Up Your Marketing Infrastructure

"If you haven't yet built something people want, great marketing will only make you fail faster." —Rob Walling, founder of Drip

Is your website ready for growth?

Picture this: you wake up tomorrow and look at your Google Analytics and it shows that 25,000 people are on your website or in your app.

Amazing. You did it!

Or did you?

Is that a good thing?

Are you prepared for that traffic? What if they did everything your website said? Would that lead them down the ideal path for conversion? Is your conversion funnel a well-oiled machine or are you just tracking your sign-up rate? Do you even have Google Analytics, HEAP, Hotjar, or Kissmetrics set up?

In this chapter, we're going to talk about the basics of designing a landing page and setting up a basic analytics tech stack. Consider this the starting point for setting up your growth marketing infrastructure. Whether you're just launching a one-page site for a new startup idea or pushing a new product for an existing company, these principles apply.

Conversion Rate Optimization (CRO) 101

Let's Talk Conversion

Are you able to convert new visitors into users or customers? It's important to start with your website (or app) before doing any marketing to make sure it's set up to convert. What that conversion goal is really depends on the goal of your website.

What do you want to happen? Do you want users to create an account, upload an image, comment on a blog post, put something in their shopping cart, enter credit card information or share something with a friend? The goal of your platform really depends on your business model.

If you run a content company (like The Huffington Post, BuzzFeed, etc.) then you want people to view lots of pages, share articles and sign up for your email newsletter. You might want to optimize the entire website for email sign-ups to retarget them. Or you could focus on content discovery to extend their session time.

For an e-commerce site (like Everlane, Bonobos, Bombas, Warby Parker, etc.), your main goal for conversion is to get people to enter their credit card information and order a product. You'll want to optimize your platform so users can check out as fast as possible and keep your shopping cart abandonment rate as low as possible—under 69%—this is the average shopping cart abandonment rate according to baymard.com.

For a community-based platform (like Reddit, Facebook, Quora, etc.) the goal is to get people to create content, engage with users or invite people to your platform. This means you'll want to optimize for activating these users as fast as possible. This could mean completing their profile or starting to submit content to your platform. This is where a strong onboarding process comes into play. Pinterest is a great example of a site with a strong onboarding process, because they use images and vivid examples to show users how their platform works.

Here's how Twitter optimized for conversion: In the early days, the company didn't have an issue acquiring users or getting its brand name out there. People were flocking to the site to claim their Twitter handles. The issue came up after people got to the website—they didn't know how to use the product.

Twitter learned that a user's satisfaction (or understanding of the product) didn't come just from sending their first tweet. Instead, it came from having a feed full of fun or interesting people posting tweets. Plus, nothing is more confusing (or depressing) than an empty Twitter feed. Twitter decided to design its entire landing page and onboarding process around getting users to follow the right people instead of getting people to publish their first tweet.

When you create a Twitter account you're asked to "build your timeline" and follow at least five users. By doing this, the first time you saw your Twitter feed it was filled with people you like, talking about things that interest you. Boom! That's a magic moment. This made Twitter become a source of go-to content from their favorite publishers or personalities. Twitter was able to improve its repeat visitors by getting people to come back just to read their Twitter feed.

How to Design a Landing Page That Converts Users

Twitter is an elaborate example of designing for conversion. Let's take a step back and start with a basic landing page. The main goal of a landing page is to educate people and then get them to do the next step listed in your call to action.

Here are five conversion tips to factor in when creating a

landing page that gets results. Basically, how to create a website that converts.

1. **Hero Image/Video:** With the main visual, use a hero image or video above the fold (this means the upper half of the front page of a website) that showcases your product or service. Tell the story of your offering's benefit with a visual. If you have a high-quality product, use the hero image to showcase the details of that product. Feel free to use images or videos to show the emotion a user will feel when using your product.
2. **Website Headline:** Clearly state the one key benefit of your product/service in the main headline. This is not to be confused with the main feature. This should be the benefit to your customer. Use the language of your customer and speak in second person. Here's an example the online food delivery service GrubHub could use: "Every Restaurant Delivered to Your Door." Notice how it uses the word "you."
3. **Copy / Subhead:** Below your website headline you should have one to two sentences about your main feature. This is where you can actually talk about your product or service. Here you can clearly explain what your product or service does. Try to avoid technical talk unless your customers use that language. Tip: use testimonials from customers to decide what language to use when explaining your product. As an example, a former company I worked for had a software product that other developers loved because they could install it in under 30 seconds. We used the line "so easy you can install in 30 seconds" and it was our top-performing landing page.
4. **Call to Action:** Add a compelling "Call to Action" button below the headline and the copy/subhead. The text on top of the button needs to be unique. Instead of just saying "sign up" or "join now" give the user a real reason to convert like "Start Your Free Trial."

5. **Social Proof:** Create a section above the fold that highlights how this product or service has benefitted your users. People might not know about your brand and they might not trust you because you're new. Instead of you trying to tell them why they should trust you, let other credible sources tell them how great it is. Use logos of publications that have written about you, logos of partners, or testimonials from happy customers.

Below is a graphic of the GrowthHit.com landing page and how it's designed for conversion with the 5 key components mentioned above. Disclaimer: this is my growth agency website.

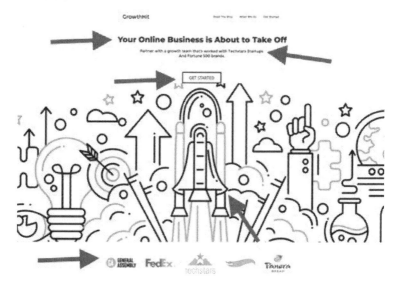

In the following chapter, we'll get into more details about how to design for conversion based on your type of business – a B2B (business to business) or B2C (business to consumer) company.

Consider this section the minimum viable product for your landing page.

Setting Up Analytics and Identifying Key Performance Indicators

Before you get that wave of one million users, you want to make sure you're tracking everything properly. Sadly, a lot of companies don't take care of this until after a launch or a surge of traffic.

This is what tends to happen with some early-stage companies.

You get some press or you start experimenting with things on the side. Something works and you get traffic to the website. It's a miracle.

Visitors hit your site and you have a nice spike in traffic. The next question is where did the traffic come from? How did they hear about us? How do we attribute sales? If you don't have the right analytics structure in place, you can't understand the data and, even worse, you can't learn from the numbers.

This is why you want to make sure everything is being tracked on your website from day one.

How do I set up my analytics?

In chapter 9, you'll find a list of options for marketing tech stacks. Let's assume that you're just starting out and you only have Google Analytics. Hey, it's free and surprisingly robust. The setup is straightforward:

Step 1: Create a free account with Google analytics and create an ID for your web domain.
Step 2: Place the Google ID on your site in the header or use a Google Analytics plug-in (Shopify and WordPress both have

plug-ins that allow you to easily do this).

Step 3: Check Google analytics to make sure data is coming in.

Great, you're getting closer.

As the data starts to come in, some questions will fill your head. What metrics should you be tracking? What metrics are you using to drive your actions? What vanity metrics are you trying to ignore but can't—I'm looking at you, page views.

Before you dive into the data, you need to know what metrics you should care about. The metrics you use to manage your business depend on your industry and your business model.

Here's a snapshot of key metrics or KPIs (key performance indicators) by industry to use to evaluate the performance of your business:

- **E-Commerce:** CAC (customer acquisition cost), LTV (lifetime value), average order price/size, conversion rate, sales per day, number of visitors, shopping cart abandonment rate, sign-up rate.
- **Content Sites:** Page views per visit, time spent on site, number of comments per post, page depth, sign up rate.
- **Community/Social Media:** Number of comments, number of ratings, number of responses, number of times shared, number of times retweeted, number of mentions, sign up rate.
- **SaaS (Software as a Service):** Churn rate, monthly recurring revenue, trial activation rate, time to close, sign-up rate.

These KPIs should be the guiding light for all of your actions. Here are some things to factor in when looking at your analytics:

- **Vanity metrics vs. actionable metrics:** A vanity metric can make you feel good, but it doesn't change your actions. Use a metric that's going to help drive your marketing and business decisions. Example: Email sign-up rate per day. How is it trending from this week to last week? A 2% decrease in your email sign-up rate may change your behavior to test new incentives for getting a sign-up, like a giveaway, a discount or an ebook.

· **Reporting vs. exploratory data:** Reporting data is important because it keeps you in the know about the daily business operations and what's going on. Exploratory data is going deeper into the data based on a hunch you have. It allows you to find interesting and unexpected insights that you might not be looking at day in and day out. For example, you might see that your purchase conversion rate is increasing but you don't know why. Taking a deeper look, you start to analyze mobile traffic from influencers and you find that they have a conversion rate that's 4% higher than your average. This gives insight into where you should be focused.

Here are some questions to ask yourself as you look at your data and try to understand what's happening on your site:

· How is this data trending compared to last week or last month?
· Which traffic source (social, email, cost per click (CPC), referral, direct, organic) results in the most conversion or longest session duration?
· How do mobile users compare to desktop users?
· How do new users compare to returning users?
· What pages have the highest bounce rate? How can you improve that page so people don't leave?

Set up a weekly KPI report to help you answer these questions on an ongoing basis. For a free template of a KPI report, go to growthmarketersplaybook.com and download the growth templates to see the top metrics I use to track traffic for my clients.

Now that Google Analytics is set up and you're looking at the right metric, the next step is URL tracking.

This is extremely important because it allows you to understand where every user is coming from and which campaigns are working and which ones are not. Customizing every URL with the right structure allows you to attribute marketing resources to online sales and conversions.

Google's campaign URL builder (ga-dev-tools.appspot.com/campaign-URL-builder/) lets you create custom URLs very easily. You can also make your own.

Tip: For your own free custom URL builder go to growthmarketersplaybook.com and download the growth templates to use the template that I created for my clients. I prefer using my own rather than Google's builder because I can create multiple URLs at once. To make your own URLs, enter in the URL of the destination page and the campaign information you need to understand what drove in the traffic. Below are the categories to fill out.

Campaign Source: Example, Facebook
Campaign Medium: Example, social
Campaign Name: Example, product_launch
Campaign Term: Example, Promocode
Campaign Content: Example, Cat_image

Once the URLs have been created and distributed, you can go to Google Analytics to filter your acquisition traffic by campaigns and see your custom URL campaigns.

It's essential to have a basic conversion funnel and your analytics platform set up before you start driving traffic to your website. Now that your marketing infrastructure is in place, you're that much closer to being able to focus on growth.

CHAPTER 6 CHEAT SHEET

- Before you start driving traffic to your product, you need to make sure you can handle it with a website, app or just a landing page that is optimized to convert a visitor into a user.
- In order to improve your site, you need to be able to learn from the data. That means having clean and accurate data. At the minimum, have at least three things in place: Google Analytics, the Facebook Pixel and use urchin tracking models (UTM) to customize all your links.
- Decide on the key metrics or key performance indicators (KPI) you're using to determine if your campaigns are working or not.

7. PLAYBOOK: How to Run Your Growth Team

"You gotta build a team that is so talented that they almost make you slightly uncomfortable." —Brian Chesky, Airbnb CEO

The top growth teams are the ones that expedite a feedback loop with their customers the fastest.

Wait, what does that mean?

That means that they run growth experiments at a rapid rate and are laser focused on using the customer data to drive their actions.

These elite growth teams run experiments, get feedback from their customers and iterate on those experiments at a rapid rate. They have assumptions and their own gut feelings about growth, but they always use data to drive their actions.

These actions are in the form of running different experiments on their product experience. It could be A/B testing landing pages with different copy or testing a new distribution channel to acquire users. These experiments can prove or disprove their assumptions. They do this every single day and are always optimizing and testing their funnels.

Simply put, your team needs to be relentless.

This is the mindset you want to take on before diving into any growth marketing channel.

Why is being relentless important? Because no matter what

company you work for, eventually you'll hit a wall and growth will slow. I was leading growth at an e-commerce startup that had just raised $4 million and our growth rate started to stall after seeing two years of constant growth month over month.

It wasn't that we weren't working hard, it was because we weren't focused and dedicated to rapid iteration.

If I was going to scale a startup the right way, I needed to apply the framework used by companies like Dropbox and Airbnb.

Here's a look at the process I used to run my growth team and scale multiple startups to over a million dollars per month. Most importantly, I explain how to power through the highs and lows of running a marketing team.

Start With the End in Mind

What is your business objective? For an e-commerce company, it's pretty simple—you should care about revenue growth. To unpack that further, you want an overall purchase conversion rate over 3% and 7% week-over-week user growth, with a customer acquisition cost (CAC) that's under $30.

What should you focus on right now? The key word here is *focus*. You can work on your conversion rate, user acquisition strategy and referral mechanism at the same time. But can you do both of them extremely well at the same time? For smaller growth teams, the answer is no. That's why focus is so important.

Brian Balfour, former head of growth at HubSpot, makes a strong case for focus in the following illustration. He says that focus leads to easier decision-making for individuals and teams. Plus, focus helps you be world class in a particular area vs. being just okay in multiple areas. Below is his graph on staying focused.

Why Focus Wins

Created By: Brian K Balfour - http://www.coelevate.com

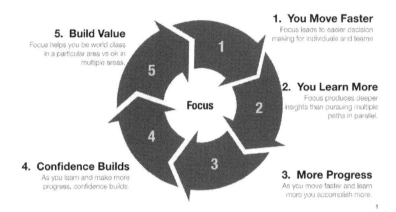

5. Build Value
Focus helps you be world class in a particular area vs ok in multiple areas.

1. You Move Faster
Focus leads to easier decision making for individuals and teams

2. You Learn More
Focus produces deeper insights than pursuing multiple paths in parallel.

4. Confidence Builds
As you learn and make more progress, confidence builds.

3. More Progress
As you move faster and learn more you accomplish more.

How to Be a Data-Driven Marketer

Focus also means focusing on fewer metrics to drive your actions. One metric should drive your entire growth team. Yes, one metric.

The goal is growth, but what is the one metric you should be focused on? Your entire team needs to be on the same page with the key metric you're focused on right now.

With an e-commerce company, the main metric could be purchase conversion rate. That means before ad spend goes up or before the company starts to invest in content marketing, the company needs to be focused on hitting the conversion rate goal of 2%. This way the team can handle an increase in traffic volume.

Once you have decided on this one key metric, the best part about this decision is that it helps determine the actions of everyone on the team. From the developer to the designer, everyone is aligned to improve this one main metric.

For example, the e-commerce company I work with felt so empowered when we decided to focus on conversion. The UI/UX team started focusing on the biggest audience with the lowest conversion rate. For us, that meant first-time users on mobile.

We started testing moving the mobile navigation to the bottom of the screen (easier to use your thumbs) and making the images load even faster.

The ad team started focusing more top-of-the-funnel ads on mobile to our low-price-point items that have the highest conversion rate.

The email team was focused on designing email newsletters that are optimized for mobile with big buttons and big images.

Everyone was focused on the same goals and after two months and about eight different experiments we were able to double our conversion rate.

Another example of how one metric drives a team's actions would be a company like MailChimp, an email service provider. They might determine that their one metric to focus on is net adds, which is the number of new customers added per month over the number of customers that churned.

As this number moves, the actions of the marketing team should move with it. If net adds goes down, that might mean that more people are churning. What do you do? Look into why they are leaving. Maybe customer service hasn't responded to various support questions. Maybe users aren't happy with your product, but the problem is they haven't upgraded to the newest version.

If the metric increases and sales go up, that would also drive more actions from your growth team. Maybe a paid ad campaign is doing really well for driving sign-ups and subscriptions, so you should increase the spend on that campaign.

Maybe your new email onboarding campaign is working or you did a 20% off promo that helped lift the numbers. Notice that as the number moves up or down it quickly helps you ask the right questions. That's a sign that you are focused on the right metric.

How can you determine your one key metric or your north star?

Here's a straightforward approach to finding the one metric that matters from the brilliant minds behind *Lean Analytics*. Below is a graphic from that book that shows what metrics you should measure based on the stage of the company (y-axis) and the industry (x-axis).

	E-commerce	2-sided market	SaaS	Mobile app	User-gen content	Media
Empathy	Interviews, qualitative results, quantitative scoring, surveys					
Stickiness	Loyalty, conversion	Inventory, listings	Engagement, churn	Downloads, churn, virality	Content, spam	Traffic, visits, returns
Virality	CAC, shares, reactivation	SEM, sharing	Inherent virality, CAC	WoM, app ratings, CAC	Invites, sharing	Content virality, SEM
	(Money from transactions)		(Money from active users)		(Money from ad clicks)	
Revenue	Transaction, CLV	Transactions, commission	Upselling, CAC, CLV	CLV, ARPDAU	Ads, donations	CPE, affiliate %, eyeballs
Scale	Affiliates, white-label	Other verticals	API, magic #, midplace	Spinoffs, publishers	Analytics, user data	Syndication, licenses

As an example, an e-commerce company that sells toys online at the virality stage (focused on acquiring new users through customer referrals) should focus on its customer acquisition cost. For that toy company, it's all about acquiring as many new customers as possible at the lowest price.

If a software as a service (SaaS) company that sells email software (a MailChimp competitor) is at the stickiness stage (focused on repeat customers), then they should focus on their churn rate. For them, it's all about designing a product experience and retention strategy that keeps people happy and coming back each month.

Your one key metric might not be on this graph, but it could directly impact one of the metrics in the graph. It could be a micro-conversion of one of these metrics. Here's an example of how Airbnb used one micro-conversion metric to scale their growth to a $24 billion valuation:

In its first three years, Airbnb really struggled to get any traction with its product of renting out your room or home. It had a small group of users that loved its product, but it couldn't break through to a big audience. Airbnb built up the supply side with listings and started to get potential renters to the site but struggled to convert them. Its conversion rate was below average and no one could figure out why.

After going through the user flow, the CEO didn't like the feel of the product. That's when he decided to test professional photography on the site instead of user-generated photos of listings. Airbnb tested this idea in the New York City market by sending out a professional photographer to the listings, and the results were staggering. The conversion rate in New York City outperformed every other Airbnb market.

That's when the company decided to launch professional photography in every market. Its metric ended up being the percentage of listings with professional photography. Airbnb's founders still credit this move as the main catalyst for their success.

Here's a breakdown of how they ran this process that transformed their business:

STEP 1: *Create an Experiment Focused on a High Impact Area of the Business*

- *Professional Photography = More Bookings*

STEP 2: *Test with a Clear Goal in Mind (Increase number of nights booked)*

- *Sent 20 Photographers to Photograph NYC Listings*

STEP 3: *Measure Results*

- *Professionally Photographed Listings > Other Listings*

STEP 4: *Use Results to Make a Data-Driven Decision*

- *Launched Photography as a New Feature*

How to Manage Your Growth Process

You've determined your main business objective and the one metric to focus on.

Now, what do you do to impact that number? How do you maximize your resources to have the biggest impact? How do you run your growth team? As a marketer, you want a general understanding of all the potential distribution channels that are at your disposal for acquiring new users.

First, let's do a summary of all the options for growth. Below are two charts that show almost everything you can do as a marketer to grow your online businesses. The first chart is from the book *Hacking Growth* and shows 27 growth experiments to run.

The second chart is from the book *Traction* and it lays out the 19 channels you can use to grow your company. Think of this as your Denny's menu for growth marketing.

27 Growth Experiments

VIRAL / WORD OF MOUTH	ORGANIC	PAID
Social Media	Search Engine Optimization	Online Ads
Embeddable Widget	PR and Speaking	Affiliate Advertising
Friend Referral Program	Content Marketing	Influencer Campaigns
Online Video	App Store Optimization	Retargeting
Community Engagement	Free Tools	Ad Networks
Giveaways and Contests	Email Marketing	Sponsorships (Blogs, Podcasts)
Platform Integrations	Community Building	Native Content Ads
Crowdfunding	Strategic Partnerships	Content Syndication
Games, Quizzes	Contributed Articles	
	Website Merchandising	

Source: Hacking Growth by Sean Ellis and Morgan Brown

19 Traction Channels

1. Viral Marketing
2. PR
3. Unconventional PR
4. Search Engine Marketing (SEM)
5. Social and Display Ads
6. Offline Ads
7. Search Engine Optimization (SEO)
8. Content Marketing
9. Email Marketing
10. Engineering as Marketing
11. Targeting Blogs
12. Existing Platforms
13. Business Development
14. Affiliate Programs
15. Trade Shows
16. Community Building
17. Sales
18. Offline Events
19. Speaking Engagements

Source: Traction *by Gabriel Weinberg*

I know, this is a lot of options. Right about now, some questions might be coming into your head as you think about where to start:

- Should I be focused on new users or existing users?
- How powerful can SEO be for my business?
- How can I optimize email to increase sales?
- Should I build a referral program into my site?
- Do I need to start a blog?
- Does PR actually work? If so, should I pay someone to do it

or do it in-house?

- Do I need a video person to make video content?

As you try to answer these questions, think about what is right for your business. What marketing channels are even an option for your business?

Your Business Model Drives Your Marketing Strategy

The amount of money you make from your online sales, online advertisements, subscription fees, affiliate partners or whatever else, directly impacts how much money you can put back into your business to get new users.

Yes, you could be a VC-backed startup that raised money specifically for marketing, so you don't have to worry about being a profitable business. Yet. You're correct for the short term, but that funding doesn't last forever.

Your marketing budget (or lack thereof) determines whether you can focus on free / cheaper channels (SEO, email, content marketing, word of mouth) or paid channels (SEM, social ads, giveaways). Your cash flow dictates the distribution channels you can test.

In addition to your business model, your stage of business determines what channels you should test. If you're still in the idea-development phase for a product or business, then you can focus on channels that don't scale, like hosting Meetup events, customer interviews and being scrappy.

If you have product-market fit and paying customers, then you can expand your marketing budget and test social ads or other paid channels.

Before you start evaluating every option, you need to understand the dynamics of what makes a marketing budget sustainable. That means understanding a user's lifetime value

(LTV), the customer acquisition cost (CAC) and how long it takes to get paid back. To summarize, it's the following three metrics:

(1) Customer Acquisition Cost (CAC)
(2) Lifetime Value of a User (LTV)
(3) Payback Time for a User

Why do these things matter? You become very powerful within your company if you know exactly how much it costs to get a user to sign up or how much it costs to get a user to make a transaction against how much that customer is worth to you over that user's lifetime.

How to Prioritize Your Growth Efforts

How do I know the main thing to focus on right now? Instead of trying to guess which marketing effort will most impact your one key metric, you can use a quantitative process with this growth scorecard to decide what's right for you.

List the top 10 growth experiments you believe will impact your key metric. Next, give those experiments a score from 1 to 5 based on the level of impact, and then another score (also from 1 to 5) based on ease of implementation. For impact, 1 means low impact and 5 means high impact. For ease of implementation, 1 means hard to implement and 5 means easy to implement.

Finally, add up those numbers to determine what to focus on right now. You want to focus on the items with the highest score.

Below is a template to use when scoring your experiments. You can access this template at growthmarketersplaybook.com and download the growth templates to build your own growth marketing scorecard.

Growth Idea	Impact (1 to 5)	Ease (1 to 5)	TOTAL
Create dynamic ads on Facebook for users who abandoned their shopping cart.	4	4	8
Optimize the product detail page for a faster and better mobile experience	5	2	7
Launch a campaign that gives first-time users a 15% discount within seven days of signing up	4	3	7
Include more social proof and testimonials on the top landing pages.	3	3	6
Create an incentive for customers to refer a friend and share on social.	3	3	6

In the above table, you can see the scores I gave various initiatives for the men's fashion e-commerce company.

For dynamic ads on Facebook, I gave it an impact of 4 because, although it's not hitting a large audience, it's hitting a very important segment—users who have just abandoned a product detail page.

For implementation, I gave it a 4 because I am assuming the e-commerce client is on Shopify so it's a very simple integration to sync a product catalogue with the Facebook Ad Manager tool. That's how you assign scores.

How to Introduce a Growth Process to Your Company

It's not easy to introduce a new process to an existing team. Any type of change can be hard to sell internally. Below are some guides and tactics on how to implement an experiment-focused growth marketing process at your company. I've broken it down into four deliverables to guide you.

- Identify your objective
- How to structure your team
- How to structure your meetings
- How to structure your week

Identifying the objective for your growth marketing team

Here's how you can break down your overall team objective to get everyone on the same page. It's important to not only get your team on the same page but to get leaders or executives in other departments on the same page. That's key if you need approval or buy in for outside teams like sales, operations, development or customer service.

Plus, this helps everyone know what metric to focus on as a team.

1. **Identify Business Objectives:**Why do we exist and what are we trying to accomplish? Example: increase # of new customers.
2. **Set Goals for Each Objective:**What does success look like? What is the outcome? Example: 5% increase in new customer emails per week.
3. **Establish KPIs:** What are the numbers that tell you if you're successful or not? Example: Purchase Conversion Rate.

4. **Create Targets:**What is the expected or desired result for the KPI? Example: Conversion Rate of 3.5%.
5. **Build Segments:**What will we analyze to see if we're successful or not? Example: Visitors by social, search, referral, direct and paid traffic.

Note: The most important tip is #4. Make sure you draw a line in the sand and pick an actual number as your target. It's essential to have clear goals your team should hit. Don't just focus by saying "hey, let's increase our conversion rate". Instead, be specific and say " We are working to hit a conversion rate over 3.5%."

How to Structure your Growth Team

Below are the key areas you want covered as you're looking to execute on your growth marketing goals. The main thing is to have a team that can execute on every growth experiment you have. Your team shouldn't be dependent on outside parties that are bottlenecks.

- **Growth Manager:**This person owns the growth objective and the main KPI that everyone is focused on.
- **The Specialist:**This is a marketing professional who specializes in the vertical for this team or project. Examples could be an SEO-focused copywriter who is creating the blog content or it could be the videographer who is mapping out the video strategy.
- **Data Analyst:**The individual who collects and organizes the data for the growth experiments. They'll build the dashboards and are responsible for presenting the data in the meetings.
- **Developer / Designer:**Technical person or designer who can execute on the digital marketing experiments.

Tip: It's okay if one person covers more than one of these roles.

For example, the growth lead could also be the person who does the job of the data analyst and manages the team.

How to structure your growth meetings

If you want to be data-driven, then it's important to start your meetings with your KPIs and the performance of your experiments.

Next, you can dive into your findings and your pipeline for the various marketing campaigns you want to run. Then end your meeting with the action items of every individual on the team and what experiments you'll do to move the needle. Here's how to do that in under an hour.

15 Minutes: Metrics Review and Update Focus Area

- Review data around the OMTM (one metric that matters)
- Positive factors vs. negative factors
- What to focus on now (short term and long term)

10 Minutes: Review Last Week's Tests

- Number of tests and what we learned

15 Minutes: Key Lessons Learned from Experiments

- Positive vs. Negative (Embrace the failures)

15 Minutes: What to Focus on in This Cycle

- Take growth idea nominations from the group based on ease of implementation and impact

5 Minutes: Action Items and Ownership

- Determine the action items to run your experiments

and—this is important—assign individual ownership to each one. Don't assign multiple people to own something. If it's not clear who owns something, then assume that no one will.

To manage the meetings, I am a big fan of Trello. Rob Sobers, head of growth at Varonis, created a Trello template for running growth that I use for all of my clients. You can find it here: https://robsobers.com/growth-hacking-trello-template/.

Tip: With meetings, it's not about what you preach but what you tolerate. Don't tolerate anything but a data-driven meeting. That's why you start with your KPIs and how they're trending.

How to structure your week

The guys at Ladder.io have created a structure for organizing your week as a growth marketer. Here's a look:

MONDAYS = Analysis

This is a day for diving into your data. Track your KPIs, measure your experiment, spot trends in the data and track your performance against your goals.

TUESDAYS = Planning

Based on your findings from Monday, what experiments can you run to hit your business objectives? Manage your experiments pipeline by taking these growth ideas and turning them into action items.

WEDNESDAYS = Approval

Work with your CEO or manager to get final approval on the growth experiment(s) your team wants to prioritize.

THURSDAYS = Execution

After getting approval, start building, designing and implementing the experiments you selected on Tuesday.

FRIDAYS = Learn

The execution will continue into Friday but it's also important to stay fresh and current by always learning. Dedicate 20 minutes to three hours to learning. Read recent case studies from your industry, take online classes to stay fresh or browse through a cutting-edge company's site for inspiration. By just dedicating a small chunk of your time to learning, you'll find that it helps you come up with even more growth experiments for your company.

What to Do When You Stop Growing

"As an entrepreneur, you have to be okay with failure. If you're not failing, you're likely not pushing yourself hard enough."
—*Alexa Von Tobel, founder of LearnVest*

No new email sign-ups. Search traffic has hit a wall. Only your aunt likes your Facebook posts. I've been there. I feel your pain.

There comes a time when your growth will slow down and it'll probably happen sooner than later. Steve Blank, Silicon Valley serial entrepreneur and coauthor of *The Startup Owner's Manual,* calls this first wall in a startup's life "the trough of sorrow." The hype of the launch and the newness of the product is gone. You're old news.

First, it's important to have something in place to keep yourself focused and, most importantly, motivated. You need to fall back on the things that got you excited enough to focus on the opportunity. Or the things that got you mad enough to solve this problem. In other words, follow the anger.

Here's how focus would work for a company like Uber: I hate cab lines. I hate waiting 15 minutes for a cab. I hate it when they don't take credit cards. And I hate how they smell. If you're marketing for Uber, then those are the things you could remember in those tough days.

Second, focus on the small group of people who actually love your product. As mentioned in chapter 4, you should only focus on growth if you have product-market fit. If you have product-market fit then you're delighting a small group of people and they're so excited that they're telling you about it.

Glorify those small wins. Share those comments and their feedback with your entire team (or just yourself if you're a team of one)! It's those little wins that will help you push through the "dark days" that are filled with flat growth, the doubters, the haters, the competitors and the voices in your head. It's those happy customers that give you hope that this product can work.

Now that you are motivated to push through, let's talk about what to actually do. It's time to start evaluating every possible marketing initiative in a smart and efficient way. We'll leverage the growth scorecard process we mentioned earlier in this chapter to evaluate which marketing channel to test.

Evaluate potential digital marketing channels

As you're going through your growth ideas, make sure you focus on the ideas that can have an impact and move the needle. Here's how to take that exercise even further:

Step 1: Write down any channel or tactic that you think will help you grow. These could be existing channels that have shown signs of hope or marketing channels you have never tested.

Step 2: Only test channels or growth tactics in order of potential impact and ease of execution. Your scores on the growth idea scorecard will help you prioritize which experiments to focus on.

Step 3: If an experiment starts to work, then you should create guidelines for the channels or ideas to make sure you maximize this channel or strategy. These guidelines could include the following for a content strategy that shows signs of working:

- What type of images and copy are you posting?
- What voice are you using when you publish to it?
- How many times are you posting per week or month?
- Who is listening to and interacting with customers?

Step 4: Allocating the right amount of time, money and resources to those channels. This way you can focus on finding the next channel or tactic to test.

Here's an example of how PayPal used experimentation to find a growth marketing strategy that worked:

When PayPal was trying to get early traction, they focused on paid ads and partnerships with banks. They quickly learned that a broad ad campaign would be too expensive to get the conversion numbers they wanted. The bank partnerships weren't moving fast enough. Sadly, big companies, especially commercial banks, aren't exactly agile.

After testing and failing with these two distribution channels, they went for a more aggressive referral program. The referral program (their third option) allowed users to get money for inviting a friend to use PayPal. This channel proved to be the marketing initiative that gave them the traction they needed to reach millions of users.

How to know which marketing channels to prioritize

Which marketing channels will have the biggest impact? How do you assign a score for impact? How much time and energy should you allocate to each growth idea? Here's what you need to factor in when prioritizing marketing ideas:

Determine which marketing channel or campaign could have the biggest impact. If you had to make a bet on one untouched marketing channel that would have the biggest impact on your company, what would it be? What would move the needle the most? Which channel would impact the biggest number of users or potential users? Which channel touches the segment of users that spend the most amount of money with you? It's those questions that should help you prioritize your marketing actions.

As an example, if you have a significant email list and you haven't implemented a robust email marketing campaign, then that's a low-hanging fruit. You could optimize your welcome email to increase your click-through rate, roll out an email drip campaign to increase email sends, launch a transaction email that emails users four hours after they left something in their shopping cart.

As another example, maybe you haven't done anything around SEO and you used SimilarWeb.com to see that your top five competitors get over 60% of their traffic from search. It could be worth optimizing all of your pages for search or rolling out an SEO-driven content marketing campaign.

Start Testing With Free Online Marketing Channels

In most cases you want to start with free channels and leverage what is working and apply that knowledge to paid channels. For example, you could be looking at paid ads vs. a content marketing initiative. After doing some keyword research (using the Google Keyword Planner tool in AdWords), you could see a strong demand for keywords around topics related to your industry.

Yes, you could start tossing money into AdWords or you could start blogging about topics around those keywords. Both will cost you something (money or time) but let your business model drive which one you do first.

Prioritize Experiments With the Fastest Feedback Loop

The most successful startups are the ones that can iterate the fastest. To dive into that even more, that means launching something, getting feedback, learning from that feedback and then iterating on that knowledge. The main word in that process is *feedback*. How fast can you get feedback to drive your next iteration?

With every failed experiment, you get that much closer to finding the right growth opportunity. Imagine you have an idea to build a new tool that you believe will be great for user acquisition for your startup. However, your product team says it'll take six weeks to go live. Then you need two weeks to see if there is any demand for this tool. That's a total of eight weeks.

Or you can go with another option where you launch a landing page in two days, then drive traffic to that page and see if people sign up to be notified when this product or service launches. This option allows you to get faster feedback about whether or not people would even want this product.

What segments are you targeting?

Which users are you targeting with your marketing initiative? Not all users are created equal. Are you going after new users? Are you looking to reengage existing users? Are you targeting your most active users or the users that spend the most money, or are you going after users who just visited your site once?

For e-commerce companies, people who have already spent money with you are much more likely to spend money with you again. You already know what they like and they have already given you their credit card information. What have you done to reactivate them?

Determine if the distribution channel is mature or emerging

Before you embark on any marketing channel, you need to know where that marketing channel is at in its lifecycle. Is it a new, emerging channel that just recently started getting traction or is it a mature platform that has reached a point of saturation?

For example, if you went all in on building an Instagram following in 2013, then you hit a gold mine. It was a wide-open channel that was growing faster than any social media platform. It had no ads, no algorithm for your main feed and no limit to how many people you could follow. However, it's very different after 2018 and it's becoming harder and harder to acquire users. It's oversaturated and you're competing with more ads, more brands and a higher standard of content.

As you evaluate social platforms, marketplaces, forums and marketing channels, understand where they are in their lifecycle. That will impact how easy or hard it will be for you to get traction.

See what your competition is doing

The more you can learn from your competitors the more creative you can be with your growth initiative. That means studying the competition to see what traffic channels are working for them. Are they getting more users through search, social, ads or referrals? What ad networks are they using? What influencers or press have written about them?

Okay, so how do you know if something isn't working or if it just hasn't been given enough time?

Your testing cycle is totally dependent on your industry, so take this advice with that in mind. For experiments, you want to allow a test to run through a normal business cycle with enough actions to get a decent amount of data. A normal business cycle could be around two weeks so you get two weekends and two work weeks of data. If you run a small startup, you want to have a minimum of 500 actions on each experiment. It might require 1,000 visits or 100,000 visits to get those actions.

Regarding traffic, organic traffic is ideal because it's authentic. But it might take a while to get the traffic volume you need. In that case, you can leverage paid traffic to accelerate your tests. Facebook Ads and Google ads are good options for getting paid traffic.

Closing Note

Before you start testing every single distribution channel, please make sure you're always focused on your ideal customer. Ask yourself the question: "Is this marketing channel right for my specific audience?" Using this customer-centric question to guide your actions is a good way to make sure your end user is always a priority.

CHAPTER 7 CHEAT SHEET

- Use the growth scorecard approach to quantify each growth idea by impact and ease of implementation. Then prioritize them accordingly.
- As a team, determine the one metric you're using as your top marketing goal. Use a data-driven approach to running your meetings and your week.
- Where can you put your resources that will have the

biggest impact? Don't get caught up in what everyone else is doing.

- Stay motivated by glorifying your happy customers—even if it's only a handful of people.
- Follow the framework for rapid experimentation to uncover the right channel or experience that will help you turn the corner.

8. PLAYBOOK: How to Acquire, Convert and Scale

"Early in a startup you need to acquire your customers for free. Later on, you can spend on customer acquisition." —Fred Wilson, Cofounder of Union Square Ventures

In this chapter, we're going to get tactical on a few key components of the conversion funnel.

Consider this chapter a knowledge transfer of growth marketing skills to help optimize your marketing funnel and where to start when you want to experiment with these marketing channels or strategies.

These recommendations are not the definitive best practices for each phase of the funnel. They're a guide to inspire you to get started with building and optimizing your own funnel.

As you start working on your own marketing strategy, you can get a head start with this playbook and apply it to your company. We'll lay out recommendations, notable case studies and top resources for continued education.

Here's what we'll cover:

1. **Playbook for Acquisition and Retention**

   ◦ Content Marketing
   ◦ SEO

- ◦ Social Media
- ◦ Facebook Ads
- ◦ Keyword Ads
- ◦ Being Scrappy
- ◦ Email Marketing

2. **Playbook for Conversion**

- ◦ Metrics for Conversion
- ◦ Activation Strategies
- ◦ Designing for Conversion
- ◦ Customer-Based Marketing

3. **Playbook for Scaling Growth**

- ◦ Scaling with "growth hacking"
- ◦ Engineering as Marketing

Content Marketing and Distribution

Content marketing is the process for creating and distributing relevant and valuable content to attract, acquire, and engage a clearly defined and understood target audience.

Translation: use your storytelling skills to get the attention of customers or potential customers.

This could be with a 2,000-word blog post that your CEO wrote on the impact of rising interest rates in Q4 or it could be a video on YouTube that shows the 10 cutest puppy GIFs of all time.

Here are all the different types of content that you could create for your business:

- · Quizzes
- · Polls
- · Infographics

- Lists
- Q&As
- GIFs
- Videos
- Slideshows
- Long-Form Content
- Thought Leader Articles
- eBooks and Guides
- Podcasts
- Videos

Why should you do content marketing?

Before diving into content marketing, ask yourself why content marketing is right for your business. What is the right type of content for your customers? Maybe you want to educate users about your industry, and an infographic is the best way to do that. Or you sell a product that is very visual, and an online video series distributed through YouTube and Facebook is the best way to showcase it.

How do you measure if content marketing is successful?

At the start, people will not read your content and then immediately click on your product. It takes time for content marketing to work. Be patient and know that it'll take at least six months to a year before you see any sort of results.

If done right, the results will come through in the form of brand exposure, brand mentions, increased traffic, increased SEO traffic (evergreen traffic), increased leads and sign-ups and, eventually, increased sales.

What should you write about?

You might have a million ideas pouring out of you or you might be staring at a blank page. Regardless, it's important to know what is the best piece of content on the web around your category. Understand what editorial angles have worked for your competitors and how shareable their content has been. This way you know what you're up against when you're building your content strategy.

That's where Buzzsumo comes into play. Buzzsumo is a web tool that allows you to see the most shared content on the internet related to specific keywords. For example, if you're writing a blog post on "digital marketing" then you go to Buzzsumo and enter in the phrase digital marketing. It will run a query and show you the most shared articles on the internet around that topic. You can filter by Facebook shares, Twitter shares, Pinterest shares, or anything else.

Study the headlines of these articles and the structure or formats they used for these posts. How long were the headlines? Did they use social proof or certain keywords? Did they format the post as a list or rank each item? Maybe they used lots of quotes and images. These details will inspire ideas for your headline and the structure of your content.

Take it a step further and read through the comments of these articles and see what people are saying. You could see some great reviews, negative reviews and comments that talk about what the article is lacking. It's that last type of review that you want to catch.

For example, if it's an article about digital marketing and the comments said they loved the Guide to Digital Marketing but wish there were more case studies, there you go. You could make a guide that's built around case studies. Once the article is completed you can come back to this comment thread and post a link to your article.

One last tip on content: **Don't make the content about you. Make the content about your customer, aka, your reader.** The more you add value to the customer, the more likely they will read the entire article and share it with their community.

As you write this epic content, think about the article from an SEO perspective. What keywords are you using in your URL structure, your headline, your copy and your image file name? These things impact how your post will rank for certain keywords. We'll talk about this more in the SEO section below.

Okay, you thought of an article idea. You researched the topic on Buzzsumo. You wrote an amazing headline. And then you hit publish. You're done, right? Wrong.

Your job is just getting started. It's time to share this digital masterpiece on any channel that could give it a boost.

Tips for Your Content Distribution Strategy

Now this might feel tedious and annoying but it's this last part that will make or break the impact of your article. You owe it to yourself and your editorial team to push this out as well as possible.

According to content marketer Sujan Patel, 80% of his traffic at When I Work came from five articles because he distributed them the right way.

Neil Patel is one of the most famous content marketers and he sends out 250 emails to individuals for every blog post he publishes. Yes, 250 emails. He asks these people to read his blog post and share it with their connections on Facebook, Twitter, LinkedIn, wherever. These aren't just random people.

Neil finds people who have expressed interest in his industry, so it qualifies them and increases the likelihood of them to share. Brian Dean, Founder of Backlinko, decided to do this same outreach approach. He finds and emails his 250 users by doing the following steps:

Step 1: Type in your content category into Buzzsumo. Example: "Beginners guide to SEO."

Step 2: Filter the results by Twitter and export the list of Twitter users in order of most followers.

Step 3: Hire a freelancer via Elance to find the email addresses for these 250 Twitter users. You can use a tool like Clearbit to discover their email address.

Step 4: Email these users by using a tool like mail merge or have your freelancer do it manually. In the email, say that you saw they shared X article (the article with shares on Buzzsumo) and you thought they would like your article. Then ask them if they would share it as well.

Tip: Only do this if you're sending emails in a personalized way that adds value. Spam emails won't work and they reflect poorly on your brand.

Targeted email outreach can have a big impact on your content distribution strategy. In addition to that, you can do other things to push your content to potential influencers and users. Here's the content distribution playbook for sharing your content:

The Content Distribution Playbook

- Send to your email list
- Share on your social media channels
- Syndicate the article on platforms Taboola and Outbrain
- Send an outreach email to people who would like your article
- If you mention influencers in your article, email them and ask them to share the article with their followers
- Submit and post the article on other platforms like Medium and StumbleUpon
- Find your topic on Quora and repost the article as an answer with your link

- Run paid ads and remarketing ads pushing the article
- Repurpose the headline and share it again in a month

Now that your content is live and you've followed the content distribution playbook it's time to monitor the performance and keep it updated. It's okay to update it with fresh content to keep it relevant.

Content Marketing Case Study: How Mint Was Acquired for $170 Million

Mint is a personal finance website that makes it very easy to manage all of your personal finances and budgets. Its product was very groundbreaking at the time and users were obsessed with it.

The problem is that it wasn't naturally viral or shareable. Users weren't tweeting about how much money they saved on groceries. Personal finance isn't something people like to share, because it's, well, personal. While they knew their product wasn't viral they knew they needed to get people to talk about their category.

Mint decided to focus on just one main channel, content marketing. They ignored everything else and decided to make the best personal finance blog on the internet by focusing on making high-quality infographics.

They created evergreen infographics, like "How Common Is Budgeting Among Americans?" and timely infographics, like "Six End of the Year Tax Tips." This content would be shared on networks like Digg and get thousands of upvotes.

Two years after launch they had 1.5 million users and got acquired for $170 million.

Content Marketing that Rides Pop Culture Trends

What happens when you're in a category that isn't exactly exciting or sexy?

Sigstr ran into this problem. Its software product allows you to make custom email signatures. Not exactly the next Tesla or SpaceX but it's great for B2B (business to business) sales teams. Sigstr was able to tie its content to something that was exciting, *Game of Thrones*. As the season finale was approaching, Sigstr launched an epic piece of content titled "If *Game of Thrones* Characters Had Email Signatures," featuring custom email signatures for their favorite and least favorite characters. The article rode the #got hashtag waves on Twitter to the top, and is still one of Sigstr's five most shared posts of all time.

Below is a look at the top content marketing resources to take your content strategy to the next level:

- Neil Patel's blog for understanding long-form content
- Buzzsumo for researching what to write about
- Contently blog for trends in content marketing
- Buffer Blog for content distribution

Search Engine Optimization (SEO)

Depending on the industry or business that you're in, Search Engine Optimization (SEO) can be very powerful. For most e-commerce websites, search is where most of the online shopping experiences start.

According to *Lean Analytics*, 79% of all online shopping experiences start in the search bar. Basically, if you're selling anything online and you're not focused on search, you're making it much harder on yourself.

Your industry might have certain keywords that could drive hundreds or even thousands of visitors. For example, a wedding dress designer that specializes in plus sizes dresses gets over 110,000 visitors per month because they've optimized for "plus-size wedding dresses." That's free traffic if you can capture it and convert it.

SEO 101: What Matters in the Eyes of Search Engines?

Optimizing for search traffic means that you want to have a high page rank for certain keywords. In order to get a good page rank for your various pages, Google puts certain weight on various factors when it's crawling your website.

Here are the various factors by weight that Google uses to rank your web pages (note that this is constantly changing):

- Domain Trust (25%)
- Link Popularity (22%)
- Anchor Text of External Links (21%)
- On-Page Optimization (15%)
- Domain Registration and Hosting (7%)
- Traffic and Visitor Performance (6%)
- Social Media (5%)

Let's simplify SEO into two categories:

(1) On-Page Optimization of Your Site: This refers to everything you can do to optimize your website for search traffic.

(2) Link Building: Getting other websites to link to your website.

Before we talk about the first category, understand which keywords you want to rank for on Google and other search engines. Keyword Planner by Google AdWords is a free tool that allows you to research monthly searches by keyword or phrase.

You could toss in the phrase "digital marketing" and see that 246,000 people type that search into Google each month. This helps us understand that people are interested in this category and are actively looking for information around it.

After you determine the keywords you want to rank for through keyword research and keyword mapping, then it's time to optimize your website for those phrases. Here are a few things to factor in when it comes to on-page optimization for certain keywords:

- *Submit Your Website to a Sitemap:* A sitemap is a tool created just for search engines. It allows you to tell a search engine when to crawl and rank your website. WordPress users can install the Google Sitemap Generator. Otherwise, you can use sites like xml-sitemaps.com to generate one.
- *Google Webmaster Tools:* Sign up your website with the Google Webmaster Tools to ensure that it's being indexed by Google.
- *Optimize Your Pages and Posts for Certain Keywords:* Include your selected keywords in the URL structure, meta description, headline, intro paragraph and throughout the content.
- *Internal Linking:* Include internal links to other pages on your site to connect pages based on keywords. Aim to have at least one to three per page.
- *Mobile-Friendly:* Make sure your website is responsive and mobile friendly. If possible, make your website AMP-compliant. (AMP means accelerated mobile pages.)
- *Other Tips:* If you have images or video on your website, make sure the file names and alt text include your keywords. Also, factor in the total word count on your page or blog post. For example, if you are writing an authoritative blog post, then your goal should be to write 1,000-plus words as opposed to 100.

Next up for SEO, how do you build up your backlink profile?

You want to have as many authoritative websites (CNN, the *Wall Street Journal*, BuzzFeed, etc.) as possible linking to your website. If Google sees these credible websites linking to your site then they know you have an authoritative website and this helps your page rank.

This is known as building your backlink profile. Backlinks can be built multiple ways. Some include getting press from online publications, guest blogging/guest posting on other websites and by submitting your website to online directories.

As an example, a startup that identified products and locations from movies, was able to use SEO to increase monthly website visits from zero to hundreds of thousands of visits in under 12 months. We saw a big opportunity in long tail search terms for phrases like "James Bond sunglasses in *Spectre*" or "winter jacket in *The Holiday*." Each of these phrases would get thousands of searches.

We ended up designing product detail pages around each product from a movie or television show with the search phrases (rather than the actual brand name) built into the headline, URL structure, meta description and the copy on the page. Also, we realized that Google Images search was a big opportunity. Naming the file images was just as important as the H1 (Headline 1) text of the copy on the page.

SEO is not a sexy initiative with quick wins. While it's not the most exciting channel it can be the most rewarding if done right. A site built on SEO traffic is the result of a thoughtful structure, a strong technical team, ongoing site maintenance and a long-term backlink strategy.

Top SEO Resources

- Backlinko by Brian Dean for tactical articles about SEO
- Moz's Whiteboard Fridays for trends in SEO

- SEMrush for powerful SEO tools
- ClickMinded's online SEO course taught by the former head of SEO at Airbnb and PayPal, Tommy Griffith
- Robbierichards.com for actionable advice on how to grow your website with SEO

Social Media Marketing: Navigating the Social Media Jungle

Snapchat. Instagram. Facebook. Twitter. LinkedIn. Quora. Reddit. Pinterest.

The list of social channels goes on and on. Should your company be on all of these channels or just one? How do you know if you're focused on the best social channel for you? The goal of this section is to help you navigate the social media jungle.

First, is social media right for your business and growth marketing plan? Understand that social channels command a lot of attention. Regardless of your industry or end user (B2B or B2C), your customers are people who are active on some form of social media. If you truly understand your audience and how to connect with them, then there is a social channel for you to test. But which one?

How to evaluate the right social media channels for your company

Before you start posting the same thing on every channel, let's take a more strategic approach. Here's a qualitative and quantitative exercise to determine which channels are right for your business.

- *Quantitative Approach: What do the numbers say?* Start by understanding what channels are working in your industry. Specifically, what channels work for your top five competitors. Make a list of your top five competitors or top five brands with customers that align with your users. Take a tool like similarweb.com or Spyfu.com and look at the traffic volume for social. For example, let's say you have an audience that's similar to the Bonobos audience—working males that are stylish and active. SimilarWeb shows that Bonobos gets 11% of its traffic from social. The next question is, what is Bonobos' top social channel? The results show that Reddit is #1 and Facebook is #2. There you go, two channels that should be worth evaluating further. For a macro approach, reference Sprout Social's Social Media Demographic Report. Here you can understand the demographic of every social channel and see where your user personas live on social.

- *Qualitative Approach: What makes sense based on your insight?* You know your customers better than anyone because you're the business owner and you interact with them. Ask yourself these simple questions: How can you add the most value to them on social media? What type of content would they want? What questions do they normally ask? If it's a lot of detailed how-to questions, then educational videos and tutorials could be great on YouTube. If you have an aspirational brand that's very visual (think GoPro) then channels like Snapchat and Instagram could be great for showcasing how to use your product with artsy videos and photos.

Based on your qualitative and quantitative research, determine the social channels that make sense for you right now. Prioritize them and determine which ones you can actually deliver on. Tip: If you're on a team with limited resources, you're going to want to do all of them, but you might not be able to do all of them well. It's okay to start with one to three.

How do you measure social media marketing success?

Start with the end in mind. It's easy to fall into the pattern of pumping out social content rather than focusing on the results. That's why you need to start with your goal in mind. What are you trying to achieve with each channel? Here are some options for measuring success with social media metrics:

- **Awareness:** You simply care about spreading the word and connecting with potential customers. You care about followers, likes and reach.
- **Conversion:** Your goal is to turn social media followers into customers with your content. Increase sales and leads. You care about your click-through rate (CTR) and conversion rate (CR).
- **Customer Service:** Use social media as a way to interact with customers—one-to-one messaging through DM or comments. You care about positive brand mentions and social shares.
- **Retention:** Social media can be great for re-engaging customers and bringing them back to your website. You care about weekly traffic from repeat users.
- **Referrals:** Turn your customers into marketers. Ask users to share your post or page with their network. You care about shares and how many friends your followers tag on a post. (Tip: Instagram comments are great for this.)

How do you track those goals? Here are some tools to use so you can analyze if you're hitting those goals.

- **Mention:** Scour the web to see if your brand or industry is being mentioned on any social platforms.
- **Simply Measured:** See how your social media campaigns drive results through your conversion funnel.
- **Google Analytics:** Track traffic that's coming in from social media.

How to design your social media strategy

Okay, you've determined your channels and set your goals. Now, how to design a content strategy that gets results? Start by getting a head start with current best practices and competitive analysis. Tip: Always lean toward content that adds value to the customer.

Begin by understanding what's working on each channel and best practices. Buffer and Sprout Social publish frequency guides every year to give you an idea of how often to post on each channel. Use this as a starting point for frequency.

Next, pick five competitors in your space and five of the most innovative companies on your applicable channels and stalk them. Yes, stalk them online and take notes. Here are the things to watch out for:

- **Frequency:** How many posts per week/month? What time of day?
- **Types of content:** How would you categorize their content? Aspirational shots, product shots (for e-commerce brands), how-to guides, inspiring quotes or typography, types of videos, thought pieces, behind-the-scenes shots, witty quotes, etc.
- **Partnerships and Guest Posts:** Do influencers take over their Twitter handle or run their Instagram stories? How do they handle partnerships?
- **Giveaways:** Do they run giveaways on their accounts? Are they promoting collaborations with other brands? What's driving their spike in likes, comments or shares?
- **Hashtags:** Especially for Instagram and twitter, what hashtags are they using or not using?
- **Engaging with People (Actually, Being Social):** How are they interacting with users? Do they talk in the comments or take the conversation to direct message? What type of content creates the most comments?

Last, sign up for the blog of every social channel you're on. To help, check out the Instagram blog. This allows you to be the first to know when they roll out a new feature. They're tech companies so they're always innovating.

Make it a priority to be the first one to test these new features. If Instagram launches its next Stories, then start experimenting with it ASAP. You never know what feature or tool could be the next great breakthrough for engaging with users.

How to execute and scale your strategy with limited resources (i.e., time and money)

After you perform this analysis, put your content ideas into categories. Try to have at least five category types of content. Create a pipeline of content for each category so you can run experiments to see if the content resonates with your network.

For example, one of my clients had a category of inspirational quotes from founders so we made 100 images of quotes. We were set on content in that category for three months.

Take advantage of a scheduling tool like Buffer, Hootsuite, Meet Edgar or Sprout Social. Plan out your evergreen content by two weeks. By getting ahead with the evergreen content, you have more time to actually be social on these channels and engage with people. With one of my clients, we have social Fridays and we spend one to two hours making content for the next two weeks.

Final Thought

The best way to know if a social channel works is by testing it the right way. Be strategic about your content and how you measure it. As a business owner or a social media leader, your time is limited and valuable so make it count when experimenting with social media channels.

- Buffer Blog for case studies on social media strategy
- AdEspresso's blog for tactical advice on running social accounts
- DigitalMarketer for trends in social media

Facebook Ads

With Facebook and Google owning almost 100% of all online ad growth, it's worth diving deep into one of these channels to help understand how to use your online advertising budget.

Here's a breakdown on how to optimize a Facebook ad and Instagram campaign from fine-tuning the campaign creative to scaling the ad spend.

The Audience

Running Facebook ads doesn't start with Facebook. It starts with your website. Set up the Facebook Pixel on your website. The pixel is a small snippet of code that you copy from the Facebook's Business Manager and drop on your site. By setting up this pixel, you can retarget any user that visited your website and then visits Facebook.

This way you can re-engage a user that has shown interest in your website but didn't convert. It's great for B2B companies running webinars that want to retarget users that got to the registration page but didn't commit. Or it's great for e-commerce companies that want to retarget customers who put something in their cart but abandoned it before checking out.

Pro Tip: To double check that your pixel is working correctly, use the Facebook Pixel Helper Chrome Extension. If it lights up blue when it's on your site then you're good to go.

Know Who You're Talking To

Knowing who you're targeting is probably the most important aspect of your Facebook ad campaign. Getting in front of the right audience can make your beautiful ads look groundbreaking. Here are the five audiences to test in order of my preference.

1. *Your Email List:* Facebook allows you to upload your email list and retarget them on Facebook and the Facebook audience network. Game changer! This will be your highest converting segment if you have a product with lots of repeat purchases. Start here.
2. *Your Website Traffic:* The Facebook pixel allows you to retarget people that visited your website. This is a great one for reengagement.
3. *A Lookalike Audience of Your Email List/Website Traffic:* This is where the power of Facebook comes into play. Facebook knows a lot about its users: the articles they like, brands they follow, content they up-vote, exes they message, everything. They're able to make a lookalike audience based on your email list or your website traffic. Facebook claims that this audience will be 90% similar to your audience and has a reach of 2 million people. It's great for scaling and finding new customers similar to your existing ones. Tip: if you have a big list then create more custom audiences based on a list of you customers with the highest AOV (average order value) or with the most purchases. Then use these lists to create a lookalike audience.
4. *Target Fans of Competitors:* Facebook has an Audience Insights tool that allows you to slice and dice segments based on your competitors, influencers and other personalized data. We recommend starting by building a segment of over five competitors that reaches over 500,000 people.

5. *Target users based on Attributes:* You can target people based on their profile and attributes. For example, if you're selling products designed for kids ages two to six, there are lots of options. You can target moms who drive minivans, moms with kids in pre-school and grandmothers. Lots of ways to test finding the right audience for your users.

Creating Ad Content: Important Tips

If you have the resources, always test at least three images or videos against each other. I actually try and do seven but three is my minimum. Some options for images include product shots, editorial shots or user-generated shots (basically, photos not taken by a pro).

The high-quality product images are the best for a very warm buyer that needs more information on the quality of your product. Social images are great for click-through rate. Videos are great for engagement and shares. If you do a video with audio, make sure you add subtitles. It can have a significant impact on conversion because it helps capture someone's attention when a video is muted.

If you don't have the capability to do video then use Facebook's slideshow feature to make a video. For me, these outperform the video ads half the time. But always test three against each other because you'll be surprised at what actually converts. If you use text on the images, make sure the copy takes up less than 20% of the real estate on the images. Otherwise, Facebook won't approve it.

Test a Lead Magnet

The top-performing ads from a click-through rate (CTR) perspective usually give the user something in exchange for a click. For an e-commerce company, that could be 20% off their first purchase or something for free with purchase. For a B2B company, you could offer a guide or a checklist in exchange for a click or an email. Just make sure those users aren't one-hit wonders.

Turn Your Press into Ads

Social proof is a powerful thing. It allows you to use the words of a credible source to promote your brand. You can do this in the form of quotes from the press, notable partners or customer testimonials. If you hit a roadblock with ad copy, start here. The language of your fans is a great starting point.

Want More Emails? Try a Lead Ad

If you have a strong email onboarding series then go aggressive with Facebook's Lead Ads. A Lead Ad serves an ad on Facebook that captures the email within the Facebook ad unit. You can use a tool like Leadsbridge to pass that email into your email service provider. For some of my clients, we were able to get emails for under $1 per email for a good stretch. This is a great deal when most of their competitors were getting email leads for $20.

How to Optimize Ads

Congrats, your ads are live!

Now what? How do you know if your ads are performing well on Facebook? Below are six metrics to track to see how they're performing. I've tossed in some basic benchmarks, but please know that these might be high or low depending on your industry or whether you're targeting a new user or an existing customer.

- ROAS: Get your Return on Ad Spend over 300% when looking at attribution from the window of 28 days after click and one day after viewing.

- *Cost Per Purchase:* Get your CPP under 30% of the LTV of your customer.
- *CTR:* Get your click-through rate (CTR) over 1%.
- *CPC:* Get your cost per click under $1.
- *Frequency:* Watch how your conversion numbers change as your frequency goes over 10 in under 30 days
- *Relevance:* You want a relevance score over 7. This is a scale of 0 to 10 showing how relevant your ads are for a particular audience.

How to Track Your Ads

When it comes to tracking the performance of your ads, it's all about your link structure. Reference chapter 6 for more information about the link builder. Assuming you have Google Analytics set up, use Google's URL builder on any link you use for an ad. This allows you to track your campaigns once the user goes from Facebook to your website. Then you can see which campaigns result in sales and which campaigns result in a high bounce rate.

What to Do When Things Don't Work

As the great philosopher Mike Tyson once said, "Everyone has a plan until they get punched in the mouth." Sadly, most of the startups I have worked with start by doing Facebook ads on their own. They put ads live and then they don't see any results. This is when you want to roll up your sleeves and really understand what isn't working and start using that information to drive your next test. Here are some quick optimization tips for getting your ads on the right track:

- *Desktop Only:* This means only showing you ads on desktops and not showing them on mobile devices. Your conversion rate is probably better when people aren't on the go.

- *Newsfeed Only:* Put the ad where their eyes are going – the middle of the newsfeed. It's more expensive but it's a better overall return.
- *No Audience Networks:* Facebook really pushes their audience network (meaning ads on other websites) but these platforms are not as engaging as Facebook and Instagram. No need to do this when you're under $3,000 a month.
- *Duration 2–4 Weeks:* Do not set the campaign as "ongoing." Give Facebook's algorithm a set time period where you want results.
- *New iPhones:* Only serve ads on the latest version of the iPhone. If they're buying the latest iPhone, they might buy your product.
- *WiFi and New Devices:* Make the setting for mobile devices that are "connected to WiFi."
- *Manual Bid & Bid Caps:* This allows you to control how much you pay per click, per purchase or per conversion. It can guarantee you won't go over a certain price. Just know that it will take longer to deploy your spend if your bids are low.

How to Scale Ads

Well done! Your ads are on fire and bringing in customers. Now it's time to put gasoline on the fire. You're taking your spend from $5 a day to $1,000 a day. That's easy, you just change the daily spend from $50 to $1,000, right? Wrong. Here are some tips on what to do:

- *Use Facebook's Auto-Increase Feature*

If you want to go from spending $50 a day on an ad to $250 a day, just tell Facebook. They have an auto-increase feature that allows them to scale your ad spend by percentage or price while still optimizing how the ads are served. This way, you alert Facebook of your increase, so they can prepare.

- *Create Detailed Segments for Your Top-Performing Ads*

Say you're spending $20 a day on your top-performing ad. Great, let's break it up even further. Make that same ad with 4 variations that change with the copy, the images, the video or the ad type. Put $20 to each of those ad sets and you just quadrupled your ad spend on the same ad.

- *Leverage Dynamic Ads*

For e-commerce websites, Facebook allows you to upload your entire product catalog to Facebook (via an Excel document or a plug-in). This way you can do product-specific retargeting automatically. Let the computer manage the 1,000 SKUs for you and serve up products that a shopper left behind.

- *Use Facebook's Rule Alerts*

Leverage the rule-alert feature within Facebook to help manage your campaigns. This feature is great because it can save you from burning money and help you allocate your budget to the top-performing campaigns in real time. For example, you can have your budget decrease by 20% if your CPC (cost per click) goes over 20 cents. You can have a rule that auto-increases your spend by 5% if your cost per website conversion is under $20. This rule allows for a cap, so it will stop once you hit a daily spend of a $300 or whatever your budget is for your campaign.

For more information on Facebook ads, checkout growthhit.com/growth/effective-facebook-ads/ to get our latest Facebook ad course.

Top Resources

- Jon Loomer's blog for staying up to date on Facebook's ad platform
- Perpetual Traffic podcast for case studies on social paid campaigns
- Adespresso for a database of top-performing Facebook ads
- KlientBoost blog for tactical advice on paid campaigns
- Facebook IQ for getting more comfortable with the platform

Search Engine Marketing (SEM)

While Facebook Ads are focused on audience-based targeting, the potential customer may not be ready to buy your product. Google Ads captures intent-based audiences and catches people when they're looking to buy something like a "Used Blue Ford Raptor".

Search engine marketing allows you to bid on specific keywords or phrases that a potential customer uses with a search engine like Google or Bing. While you could use your SEO strategy to rank for those keywords for free, SEM allows you to pay for those clicks. But what keywords should you go after?

Google's Keyword Planner tool allows you to figure out what keywords are right for your business. You input the keywords or phrases into the tool and it'll show you the number of monthly searches for that phrase and provide the average cost to bid on that phrase. For example, the phrase "marketing plan" gets over 78,000 searches per month and it costs around $1.38 per click for that search.

Paying for clicks doesn't make sense for every industry or business because the cost per click and the return on that ad spend don't add up. If you're at a startup in the mortgage industry and you want to rank for the phrase "interest rates" then you'll quickly realize each click will cost you $20 to $30. For bootstrapped founders, this paid marketing channel could put you out of business pretty fast.

Don't want to lose market share to your competitors? Make sure that you're bidding on your brand name to protect your brand from any other companies that are trying to steal your traffic.

Top Resources

- Single Grain's blog for Google Ad strategies
- Think with Google for Partner stories on using Google Ads
- KlientBoost's blog for what's trending in Google Ads

Being Scrappy

Now we're going to break down the most underrated marketing practice of all: being scrappy. What does scrappy mean for a marketer? Scrappy is when you will roll up your sleeves and do whatever non-scalable action it takes to grow and get traction.

Most people just want to look for a silver bullet that doesn't exist, one growth tactic that will solve all their problems. The true silver bullet is actually the complete opposite of that. It's a relentless focus on getting stuff done every single day.

My first measure of potential success with a founding team is if they are scrappy. Are they willing to do the dirty work and make something out of nothing?

A Guide to Being Damn Scrappy

An early-stage company with a newly launched product probably doesn't have a lot of users yet. The good thing about that is you can do things that don't scale. You can be scrappy. You can personally touch every single new customer.

"It's better to have 100 people [who] love you than finding a million who just sort of like you. Build your business one person at a time." —*Paul Graham, Y Combinator cofounder*

That also means you need to be relentless in your hustle. It's about doing whatever it takes to make sure you have a product people love and know about, and tracking down potential users wherever they might be located, online or offline. Doing things that don't scale is absolutely worth your time and energy in the early days.

To help with your hustle, here is a step-by-step guide from Noah Kagan, CEO of Sumo. He's done this three times with Mint, V11 Media and App Sumo, so he knows what he's talking about.

1. Make a great product. But y'all know that, so I'll just dive into the tactics.
2. Create your target marketing sheet. See his example at https://okdork.com/quant-based-marketing-for-pre-launch-start-ups/.
3. Partner with similar companies and create benefit for them to email their free users.
4. Reach out to offline Meetup groups who generally have 200-to 1,000-person mailing lists.
5. Befriend owners of Facebook pages and see if you can do contests for an in-kind trade.
6. Go to the subreddit (page on Reddit) related to your business and leave comments.
7. Search 5 to 10 keywords related to you on Google and leave comments on the pages you find.
8. Give away free content or ask partners—like I did with My Travel Hacks and Free Luggage for Your Next Adventure

(Part 2).

9. Go write guest posts for any site that's related. Use Technorati or ask your existing customers which sites they like to go to.

10. Email the existing users you have asking for them to refer other people. This sounds obvious but hardly ANYONE does it. It helps if your product doesn't suck ass.

11. Leave video responses on popular related YouTube videos.

12. Manually reach out and connect with your first 1,000 customers. Likely they are MORE important than the 99,000 next people you'll get.

13. Raise your prices so you don't need to get so many people. ?

14. Manually reach out to the Twitter/Facebook followers of your competitors.

15. Look at new channels that have less competition (rules), like Snapchat, Pinterest, Instagram, to drive traffic

16. Consider going international where traffic is cheaper (okay, you're not paying, but you know what I'm saying).

17. Evaluate doing mobile-related marketing since it's more affordable (less competition).

18. Get featured on AppSumo.com, DailyWorth.com, Thrillist, Groupon or some site that promotes others.

If you're a bootstrapped founder or part of a marketing team that's just getting started, then this might be the best place to start. It's not scalable but it can help you understand where you should be focused.

Top Resources

- Noah Kagan's personal blog okdork.com
- Casey Winters's personal blog caseyaccidental.com
- *Hacking Growth* by Morgan Brown and Sean Ellis
- Sujan Patel's personal blog

Email Marketing

There are lots of ways to get people to your website. Organic search, paid search, press, direct traffic, social media, content marketing through blogs and many more options. But how do we get those people to come back? You have some options with remarketing ads, push notifications, SMS, email and more. Let's dive into the most powerful one: email.

"Retention is the single most important thing for growth." —*Alex Schultz, head of growth at Facebook*

In most cases, email is your #1 option for retention. It's a channel that people opt in to, giving you permission to send messages straight to their inbox. While it's become oversaturated with email marketers and made less powerful with Google breaking up your inbox into folders (primary, social, promotions), email is still powerful. The standards are just higher, which means you need to deliver quality if you want to make it through the noise.

At a high level, your email strategy can be broken down into three categories:

1. Email newsletters
2. Email flows
3. Transactional emails

Email newsletters are the emails that you send based on your content calendar and marketing campaigns. Examples include Black Friday email promotions, product-launch emails and weekly email round-ups. These are great for keeping your subscribers up to date on what is going on with your business and product.

Email flows are a series of emails that are sent based on what a member has done. As an example, a welcome email flow is a series of emails that a new subscriber gets when they sign up for your email list. The flow could look like this:

- Email 1: Welcome Email (Immediately)
- Email 2: About Our Product (Day 3)
- Email 3: Testimonials and Social Proof (Day 7)
- Email 4: Giveaway or Guide (Day 10)
- Email 5: Case Study (Day 14)
- Email 6: Special Promo (Day 20)

Transactional emails are emails that are triggered based on a member's profile or actions. One of the most opened transactional emails in your inbox is from Facebook. It's the email you get that has the subject line "You've been tagged in a photo." This happens when someone posts a picture of you on Facebook. You get an immediate email about it, then you click on it to see the photo because, well, it's impossible not to.

PayPal has an equally powerful transactional email when someone sends you money. This action immediately triggers an email with the subject line "Someone sent you money" and you open it to claim your cash. When done right, these emails are very powerful.

Here are metrics you can use to monitor your email campaigns:

- Open rate (% of people who opened your email)
- Click-through rate (% of people who clicked on a link in your email)
- Conversion rate (% of people who opened your email, and then made a purchase on your website)

Now, it's natural to see some churn with your email list and to see users unsubscribe. But there are things you can do to make sure you maximize the performance of your email campaigns.

Identify the best window for conversion by day. Test the days of the week you send and test the time of day you send. I have had good experience with 9 a.m. send times for some audiences and 3 p.m. send times with other audiences. See what's right for your business by testing it yourself.

The other big item you can experiment with is the subject line. I recommend A/B testing every single email subject line. Here are some testing guidelines for email subject lines:

- Shorter is better: Test using less than five words when possible.
- Personalization: Use a customer's name to get their attention.
- Second person: Test using the word "you" to make the content about the user.
- Visuals: Test using an emoji to catch their attention.
- Keywords: Anchoring around keywords like "free," "20% off," "secret," "first access" or the name of an influencer they respect can help.
- Numbers: Test using numbers when possible.
- Editorial angle: Strongly recommend leveraging persuasion techniques from the book *Influence* by Robert Cialdini in your subject lines. Tactics like scarcity, social proof, hype and authority are great for tests.

As your list begins to grow, segment your subscribers based on their behavior or attributes. Some people would love an email from you every day, and others might prefer an email on a weekly basis. Allow these users to pick their email frequency preference on their profile or you can use their open rate percentages to guide how often to send emails. Also, think about how you can use a person's gender or physical location to add value with user-specific content.

For e-commerce companies, email is the most coveted channel because traffic from email usually has a conversion rate that's more than double the conversion rate of traffic from paid channels. Use the channel wisely and it can help push your customers down the funnel to make a transaction.

Top Resources

- MailCharts for examples of top email campaigns
- Hubspot's blog for great email automation examples
- Email Monks for email best practices
- Email Insights to track the email campaigns of your competitors

Conversion

Congrats, you got users to your site!

Now what?

Are they doing what you want them to do? Are they converting? Whether that's reading a blog post, watching a how-it-works video, creating a profile, filling out a form or actually entering in their credit card information and hitting "buy."

We'll dive into some of the different tactics you can use to convert traffic, but you want to be very clear with the metric you're using to measure success for conversion. The metrics you care about will vary based on your business model or industry. Here are some general conversion metrics to consider:

- Form completion rate
- Email sign-up rate
- Profile completed
- Purchase rate
- Video view competition rate

If you're at an e-commerce company like Allbirds or Everlane then you might care about the following for your online store:

- Average order value
- Shopping cart abandonment rate
- Repurchase rate

For a content platform like BuzzFeed or Refinery29, your idea of conversion could also include the following:

- Time spent on page
- Average session duration
- Page depth
- Comments per post

For a SaaS (Software as a Service) company like MailChimp or Vidyard, your idea of conversion could include the following:

- Demo Requests
- Free Trials Started
- Upgrade Rate
- Webinar Sign Ups

Now that you have your conversion goal in mind, let's look at some options for improving that number. In chapter 6, we talked about best practices for landing pages. Assuming you have that key piece of site infrastructure set up, we'll get into how to build on top of that.

How do you convert traffic into subscribers?

It's time to convert.

That means turning a new website visitor into a qualified lead, a subscriber or someone that can help monetize your product. In most cases, this means getting them to give you their email address.

What are the tactics you can use to get someone's email address? First, make an amazing product or service they want to get email updates about. Next, you can try these options.

- **Content upgrade:** Create a piece of content (a guide, an ebook, a checklist, an infographic, anything a user would want to save) and offer it to that person in exchange for their email address.
- **Early Access:** If you're constantly launching new products or services, offer early access to your next launch.
- **Discount:** Give users and incentive for getting on your list, like 10% off or $20 toward their first purchase for signing up.
- **Giveaway:** Create a promotion around your offering and let people sign up for a chance to win. Personally, I am not a big fan of giveaways, but they actually work very well.

As an example, Koala Mattress is very aggressive with its activation strategy. The company sells mattresses directly to consumers through its online store and knows users must be converted within days of visiting the site. Mattress transactions are very infrequent and, in most cases, they happen when you absolutely need a bed and ASAP.

This is why the company is aggressive. Within 25 seconds of visiting the Koala Mattress site, you'll receive a pop-up that offers you $100 off of your first purchase just for signing up. This is one of the reasons why Koala was able to get to over seven figures in sales within its first 12 months.

With some platforms, you want more than just an email address. You actually need a user to take multiple actions and move down the funnel. This could be anything from filling out a profile for a social site to going to the product detail page for an e-commerce site.

How to Funnel a User

After you have an email address, you're on to the next step: getting the user down the conversion funnel.

For an e-commerce product, that means getting them to a product detail page to make a transaction.

For a SaaS (Software as a Service) product, that could mean getting the user to do a demo or a webinar so they truly understand if the product or service is right for them.

For a community site, it could be getting them to complete their profile and starting to engage with a community.

With e-commerce products, priming the user from the aspirational mindset (how they will feel after seeing your ad or a sharable video) to a buyer's mindset is key. This can be done through an email campaign, a remarketing campaign or a landing page on your website. The following messaging components are key to **getting a user into a conversion state of mind**:

- *Details on Quality and Price:* Give only the details a user needs to know to make a purchasing decision. Make sure the details include benefits to the user and the quality of the product, so they outweigh the price. Make it very clear. If you have an item that has a high price point then you want to educate them early on about the quality.
- *How It Works:* Provide details through a video or a number scale (Step 1, Step 2, Step 3, etc.) on how to use a product or service and what to do next.
- *Testimonials and Reviews:* Leverage quotes from your top customers or industry publications to tell people why they'll love your product or service.
- *User-Generated Content:* Showcasing real people using the product on social media is great for giving your

product the right brand lift.

If you're successful, then you've navigated the user from a home page or landing page to a page down the funnel. You're just a few clicks away from your goal.

Here are some **best practices and tactics to use for conversion.**

Product Detail Pages for e-Commerce Sites

It starts with the images. Are they high enough quality that users can zoom in on them, but not so big that the images are slow to load? Also, can you add a video showcasing how the product works or highlight the quality and various applications?

Next, you'll want to be very clear about the name of the product, the measurements and materials that make up the product. If possible, offer free shipping and free returns. These have become common practices in the new Amazon world.

Include any noteworthy reviews or testimonials about the product and, if you're in the fashion space, try adding some UGC (user-generated content) photos. All of this should be easy to read and view on desktop and mobile.

Last, make sure you accept the right form of payment for your user. Depending on your demo, that could be PayPal, Venmo, Apple Pay and/or credit cards.

For service companies or SaaS companies with a high price point, the goal might be to get a user to sign up for a demo, enroll in a webinar or just complete a contact form. If that's the case, reference the best practices from the landing page recommendations in chapter 6. If you want to take your conversion to the next level, you'll want to focus on the next chapter where we talk about customer-based marketing.

Top Resources

- ConversionXL blog for trends in website conversion
- BounceX blog for detailed guides and case studies on converting traffic
- Unbounce blog for technical advice on designing for conversion
- Crazy Egg blog guides on using heat maps and recording to understand why users aren't converting

Customer-Based Marketing

Right now, people are visiting your site. New users. Existing users. Users from ads. Users from blog posts. Why should you treat every person the same?

What if you could personally guide each user through your product with a custom and personalized experience based on what they're interested in? With the customer-based marketing infrastructure in place, you can do that.

Customer-based marketing can potentially have the biggest impact on conversion for your company. Whether you're at a B2B company or a B2C company, you're collecting data on specific customers that you can use to add value to them. Why should your most loyal customer get a pop-up about joining or see a section that asks them to sign up? They should be informed of your latest product feature, an exclusive offer for VIPs or receive content that will push them down the funnel.

First, it starts with your data and your overall marketing tech stack to make sure all of your tools speak to each other. This process is getting much easier thanks to a few impressive (and cost-effective) tools like ConvertFlow, RightMessage and Optimizely X. Read more details about these tools in chapter 9.

Here are two examples of how customer-based marketing could work for your platform:

For a creative agency looking to build more clients, a customer-based experience would go like this:

- VISIT ONE: Visit the site from a referral source (for example, the web page for the podcast blog of Entrepreneur on Fire). The landing page would have a custom image and a custom headline based on this referral source. It might mention that this service was used by the host of Entrepreneur on Fire. There might be an immediate pop-up that offers this first-time user an ebook about how to pick the right agency.
- VISIT TWO: On their second visit to the site this same user would get an exit intent pop-up (this is a pop-up that is triggered on the site when your mouse cursor scrolls to the exit corner), but it would be to schedule a free consultation because we know the user has visited the site before. This message would come in the form of a chat feature in the bottom right corner that uses personalized messages based on the data a customer gave them on the first experience. "Hey, Matt, schedule a time for a free consultation."
- VISIT THREE: After a customer schedules a consultation and visits the site, their next experience could involve a special offer of one month free or reinforce the ROI clients have by using this service. The main goal at this stage is to get the client to convert.

The conversion experiments for the second interaction and third interaction are where the real value of customer-based marketing comes into play. Being able to do promotions for the middle-of-the-funnel goal and bottom of the funnel to users that are actually at that stage. It's the right message at the right time to the right user.

Some customer based marketing tools like ConvertFlow and RightMessage, claim seeing conversion go to over 40% on certain steps because they're so good at targeting.

Top Resources

- RightMessage Learning Center for customer-based marketing 101
- ConvertFlow blog for case studies
- Optimizely X blog for current best practices on CRO and personalization
- BounceX database for case studies and behavioral marketing guides

Scaling Growth (aka, "Growth Hacking")

You have product-market fit and you have created a marketing funnel that works.

Now, how can you increase your marketing results by a factor of 10 by scaling a growth channel or by turning your customers into marketers?

By turning customers into marketers you're making it easy for your top customers to tell other people about your product or service. Some would suggest that this is where a "growth hacker" comes into play.

I don't love that phrase because of the connotation that is associated with "hacking"—it sounds like a quick and dirty shortcut. Ah, how I wish it were. But I do love the principles that go into the phrase growth hacking.

What Is Growth Hacking?

It's a buzzword that people like to toss out there. But if you take a step back, the core principles that go into growth hacking are pretty spot-on for today's digital marketing world. The skill set of a true "growth hacker" could be the game changer your company needs to start growing the right way. That's why you might care.

Now, let's start from the beginning.

In 2010, Sean Ellis, who was then the head of growth at Dropbox, was looking for his replacement. None of the marketing candidates were cutting it. That's when he decided that he needed a "growth hacker."

Backstory: Sean lead the Dropbox growth team that came up with the referral marketing engine pictured below. In a nutshell, you could pay for Dropbox or invite friends and continue to use its cloud storage software for free. This one referral mechanism was its #1 driver of user acquisition.

As Sean was looking for his replacement, he decided he didn't need a vice president of marketing. He needed someone to solely focus on growth. He needed a growth hacker.

"A growth hacker is a person whose true north star is growth. After product-market fit and an efficient conversion process, they find scalable, repeatable and sustainable ways to grow the business."

A growth hacker needs to have three things: An understanding of the principles of digital marketing, to be data driven in their actions, and lastly, to have the basic skills of a product manager.

In other words, the skill sets that make up this savvy marketer are the following:

1. Digital Marketing Fundamentals
2. Data-Driven Leader
3. Product-First Mindset

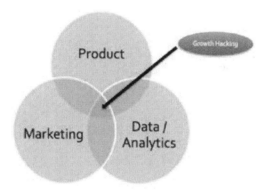

Another way to put it is that a growth hacker builds distribution into the product. Distribution shouldn't be an afterthought once the product is built. The product should be built with distribution in mind.

This phrase started to make sense but what really made it resonate with me was the idea of distribution. Growth hacking is when you build distribution into the product experience. Essentially, it's a person or team that seamlessly weaves their growth mechanism into the product.

To put more color around the idea of scaling growth through

growth hacking, here are four examples on how other companies have done this very well:

Hotmail: Turn User Emails into Mini Billboards

Hotmail was one of the first webmail solutions. It was a great product, but had trouble getting traction. The marketing team tested banner ads and even contemplated billboards. But traditional marketing wasn't working for them. They weren't getting the kind of traction that would create a sustainable business model.

Then Hotmail's VC firm came up with the idea of customizing the email signature of every Hotmail user to say "PS: I love you. Get your free e-mail at Hotmail." These emails wouldn't hit a huge number of people with any one email. Most emails are one to one. However, it's a very high-frequency distribution channel (you send multiple or hundreds of emails every day) with prime placement. Most people read the full email when it's sent from a friend, so it was guaranteed to get people's attention.

After this email signature launched, Hotmail grew to 12 million users in 18 months. This rapid growth caught the eye of Microsoft, who later acquired Hotmail for $500 million.

Another more recent example of this is how Flipagram does a similar version of referral marketing on Instagram. In order to use its slideshow feature on Instagram for free, you have to allow the "Flipagram" watermark on the images. The result: you get a free slide share tool and Flipgram gets to showcase its brand to all of your followers that watch the slideshow. Today, Flipagram is valued at over $300 million.

In the examples of Hotmail and Flipagram, these companies knew their users where on email and on Instagram. The best way to target new users was through users of the product. And if your value proposition is strong enough, users won't mind this type of referral marketing.

LinkedIn: Turn User Onboarding into a Growth Engine

LinkedIn is a social network for professionals (I'm sure you're familiar with it). When its professional network launched, it didn't initially take off at the rate of a Facebook or Instagram. So the marketing team had to really understand how to create a powerful growth engine. They determined that the most valuable tool to a user is their network. The more connections you have, the more networking and business opportunities come up.

They wanted to use this value proposition as their growth mechanism. During the LinkedIn onboarding process, they added the option to upload your contacts to see who you already knew on the platform. This allowed LinkedIn to quickly take users from five connections to over 50 connections. Suddenly, your LinkedIn profile started becoming your go-to resource for networking. Additionally, LinkedIn launched a transactional email campaign that notified you when a contact made a career change. These email triggers served as a powerful retention mechanism for bringing people back to the platform. LinkedIn went on to be acquired by Microsoft for $26 billion.

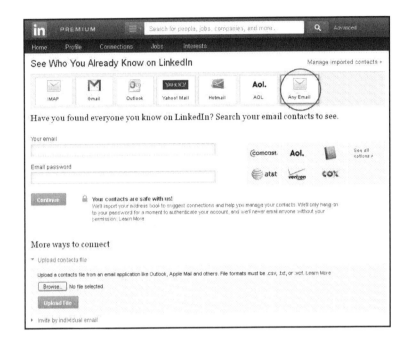

Evernote: Maximize an Unlikely Distribution Channel

As mentioned earlier in chapter 3, when Evernote launched its mobile app it was right as the Apple App Store was starting to take off. Evernote was featured on the front page of the app store. The result was thousands of downloads within one day. After that, Evernote's new product launches were always timed with any new mobile phone or new product release. The Apple app store was a new distribution channel. The CEO said:

"We really killed ourselves in the first couple of years to always be in all of the app store launches on day one."

The hard work paid off and Evernote averaged 19,000 new sign-ups per day.

Wandertab: Engineering as Marketing

Hitlist is a travel site that offers you the cheapest airfare if you're up for going anywhere in the world. Great idea, but it's in a very competitive market. I wouldn't want to go against the marketing budgets of an Expedia, TripAdvisor or Priceline.

They knew that traditional marketing channels like pay-per-click and SEO wouldn't work. Its head of product came up with the idea to create a Google Chrome extension (pictured). The extension, Wandertab, shows you a photo of travel inspiration and a flight deal to get there (based on your location) with every new tab. The extension was featured in the Chrome store, and then it was voted #1 on ProductHunt. This new product became the top driver of new users.

Wandertab
Satisfy your wanderlust with every new tab

Add Wandertab to Chrome

Harry's: Getting to 100,000 Potential Customers Before Launch

Harry's is a subscription razor company created by one of the co-founders of Warby Parker, Jeff Raider. Leading up to the launch of Harry's, Jeff wanted to build up the excitement but didn't want to throw money at advertising.

He decided to create a waitlist that had a referral mechanism with tiered incentives. After a user signed up, Harry's asked you to share the waitlist with your friends in exchange for products. The more people you invited the more products you got. Below are some of the tiers:

- Invite 5 friends: Free shave cream
- Invite 25 friends: Winston shave set
- Invite 50 friends: A year supply of free blades

The pre-launch campaign results in over 100,000 new emails and over 1,500 people invited 10+ or more friends.

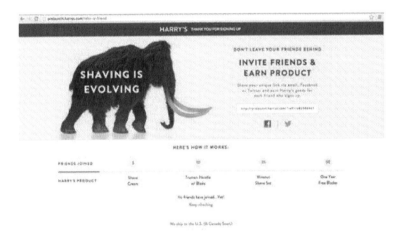

How to Apply Growth Hacking to Your Business

After you have built a sustainable growth marketing funnel, the next question is how can you rapidly increase the number of new users to your platform? For a lot of these companies, they did this by uncovering the "magic moment" of their product or service and at that point they ask users to invite their friends. Thus, turning customers into free marketers.

For LinkedIn, this was during the onboarding. For Dropbox, this was after using the product for a while. Both companies were able to identify the right time to ask customers to invite people. For e-commerce companies, you've probably seen the referral emails come in right after you make your first purchase. Example: Thanks for your purchase! Invite a friend and get a $25 credit if they make a purchase.

Another option is identifying the right channel for scalable growth. For Evernote, they were able to optimize the product release schedule to constantly be featured on the front page of the Apple App Store. This resulted in waves of free traffic and users.

For Wandertab, they were able to find an underutilized channel like the Google Chrome extension marketplace and capitalize on it as a free channel by creating a product for its potential customers. They combined engineering as marketing with an untapped distribution channel.

Another classic example of engineering as marketing is also in the form of the mortgage calculators that brokerage firms make to acquire real estate customers. This tool becomes a great lead-generation mechanism for companies.

Whether it's building the growth engine into your product, finding an untapped channel, or making a product that serves as a growth tool, it's about experimenting with different ways to acquire customers at scale.

This way you aren't dependent on paid channels or channels that don't scale.

Top Resources

- Growthhackers.com forum for case studies and AMAs from leading growth hackers
- Growthhit.com blog for insights
- Casey Winters's blog about long-form content
- Rob Sobers's blog for tips on running growth
- Brian Balfour's blog for growth hacking framework

9. RESOURCES: Finding the Right Marketing Tech Stack for You

"A growth hacker is someone who has thrown out the playbook of traditional marketing and replaced it with only what is testable, trackable, and scalable. Their tools are e-mails, pay-per-click ads, blogs, and platform API's instead of commercials, publicity and money" –Ryan Holiday, Author of Growth Hacker Marketing

It's time to give you superpowers.

Whether you're on a team of 20 or a team of one, you need the right tools to measure your performance and optimize your efforts.

Below is a breakdown of the digital marketing tools you can use to support your growth marketing efforts.

Think of this chapter as a database for building out your marketing tech stack. You can pick a few of these to build out the right tech stack for your company – they range from free tools to high-priced platforms.

Where Should You Start?

Before we dive in, I want to talk about how to think about these options. As a founder, you can easily get caught up in the nuances of the various shiny new marketing tools. In the early days, I found that the quest for the best dashboard or conversion tool resulted in information overload and lots of wasted time.

Start with the end in mind. What are you trying to accomplish and what metrics help determine if you are getting there? That will tell you which platform you need. For an e-commerce company, you need a tool that shows attribution by marketing channel (how are my Facebook ads doing?) and segmenting a conversion funnel based on a user's attributes (how are the new users doing on iOS devices vs. the desktop users?).

Below are some of my favorite tools and the right use case. I also listed similar alternatives for some of the tools listed, because there is usually more than one right solution.

For Tracking Website Traffic

Tool: Google Analytics.
A great tool for tracking where users are coming from (social media, search, email, etc.) and it's great for seeing what your traffic is doing on the site. Plus, it's free and it's powered by Google.
Use Case: Track your traffic from Google ads and Facebook paid campaigns by using custom UTMs to correctly attribute paid ads to conversion on your website. This allows you to answer which campaigns resulted in sales.

For Event Tracking

Tool: Heap.
Ideal for event-based tracking, funnel analysis and detailed retention modeling by cohorts. Heap allows you to easily track any event on your website (Example: a button click) or segment users based on a combination of actions. This tool allows you to understand how specific users behave within your website or

app.

Use Case: Onboarding is essential for apps, and Heap gathers all data during registration to make signing up simple and painless. You can track where users drop off or run into a bottleneck.

Similar Options: Mixpanel and Amplitude

For Landing Page Experiments

Tool: Unbounce
A landing page builder that doesn't require any involvement from a developer. It's mobile and web responsive and allows you to easily A/B test and optimize for conversion.

Use Case: Create different landing pages for ad traffic to test who has the highest sign-up rate or click-through rate. For example: you could test a "How it Works" video in the hero section vs. an aspirational image of how the product will make you feel.

Similar Options: Leadpages and Optimizely

For Personalization

Tool: RightMessage
Personalization software is great for making custom funnels for users based on where they are in the journey. This can be applied to B2B and B2C companies.

Use Case: You want to market to your VIP customers about a premium service for limited customers. You create a custom landing page that uses their name and targets them with early access to this premium service at a discount for VIPs.

Similar Options: ConvertFlow and Optimizely X

For Email Capture

Tool: Sumo
An exit intent email-capture tool that allows you to easily A/ B test what your email pop-up will look like. Sumo easily

integrates with any email service provider, like MailChimp, Campaign Monitor or Pardot by Salesforce.

Use Case: For all new users, you can test an email pop-up after 20 seconds. Option A shows a discount of 20% off your first purchase and option B allows a new subscriber to enter a giveaway.

Similar Options: OptinMonster and JustUno

For an Email Service Provider

Tool: Campaign Monitor

A user-friendly email service provider that allows you to create email newsletters, custom email flows and transactional emails. Campaign Monitor has an approachable price point similar to MailChimp and has a lot of powerful features for custom flows. It's a good tool for starting out.

Use Case: You want to create a five-email onboarding series for people who just downloaded your ebook. Use this tool to A/B test all email in the flow, and you can make the emails conditional based on a user's actions.

Similar Options: For e-commerce companies, I would recommend looking into Klaviyo and Bronto. For SaaS products or service companies that want to use customer data to drive their email strategy, check out Drip, Hubspot, or Marketo.

For UX (User Experience) / Heatmaps

Tool: Hotjar

A website heat map tool that records sessions of your users on mobile and desktop. Great for understanding exactly how people are using your website and interacting with your product. The tool helps you understand how various page designs are performing.

Use Case: You're launching a new product page for your company and want to create recordings and heat maps for 1,000 sessions on this page. Hotjar allows you to see how users are responding to your new design by watching those site recordings.

Similar Options: Crazy Egg and Mouseflow

For Competitive Analysis

Tool: SimilarWeb

A digital marketing intelligence platform that allows you to understand the traffic of your competitors. Everything from traffic medium to the exact keywords and ad platforms that a competitor uses.

Use Case: You want to understand how a competitor gets traffic to help determine how to build your marketing campaign. SimilarWeb shows you that 30% of your competitor's traffic is from social media. Digging deeper, you uncover that Reddit (not Facebook) is their top social channel.

For Content Marketing Research

Tool: Buzzsumo.

This tool allows you to research topics based on the number of social shares an article received. You can also research influencers and writers based on keywords relevant to your own content.

Use Case: You're researching ideas to write about for your blog. After typing three topics into Buzzsumo you uncover a topic that has five times more shares from notable influencers in your industry. Bingo – you found your topic.

For Social Media Management

Tool: Buffer

A social media scheduling tool for planning, calendaring and posting on multiple social channels from one main tool.

Use Case: If you're approaching the holiday season and don't want to be living in your social accounts, then schedule all your posts ahead of time, so you can actually engage with your

community when the post goes live.
Similar Options: Hootsuite, Sprout Social and Meet Edgar

For Ad Reporting

Tool: ReportGarden
Reporting software built for marketing agencies that merges AdWords and Facebook's Ad Manager into one platform so you can make custom reports for your clients or your own company.
Use Case: Want to show the ROI for an AdWords holiday campaign and a new Facebook video ad? You can build a custom report that shows the total spend, clicks, conversions and ROI for each channel.

Summary

This just scratches the surface of all the marketing analytics tools that are out there. It takes some research and planning to get the right stack setup, but don't make it harder than it needs to be. Use these recommendations as a loose guide for how you should approach creating the right marketing tech stack for your company.

If you feel overwhelmed, then check out the $9 marketing tech stack by Rob Sobers. He has a 2,000-word blog post that will walk you through how to find the perfect tech stack. I found it to be very helpful.

CHAPTER 9 CHEAT SHEET

- *Build your tech stack based on your business model, your budget and the metrics you care about. Start with the end goal in mind.*
- *Before investing in a marketing analytics tool, write down all the KPIs you want to track and what you want the tool to deliver.*

10. SELF-HELP: Shut Up and Grow

"The things you regret most in life are the risks you didn't take." —Farhan Masood, technology investor

Congrats, you made it to the end (or you skipped ahead).

Regardless, you're here and you have this book. Now it's time to get started and put the tips from this book into action.

Whether you're a founder or looking to get into growth marketing, take the first step and start applying the ideas in this book to your company or a side project. **Don't make excuses. Excuses are momentum killers**.

To help get those out of your system, here is a list of every possible excuse you might use. Let's get this over with right now.

Excuses Checklist

- Not enough experience
- Not enough time
- Not smart enough
- Not a business person
- Too old
- Too young
- Don't have a partner
- Not technical
- I have a kid
- I don't have enough money

- I don't have the resources
- I don't live in San Francisco
- I'm waiting for the idea to come to me in my dreams

It's easy to say that you're working hard or that you're busy working on the idea, but are you really? Are you focused on the one thing that can have the biggest impact on growth? Are you executing a plan that can have a big impact?

Or are you living in email chains going back and forth on your new logo. Are you sitting on the couch with your laptop, about to work . . . but you've had *Breaking Bad* on for two hours?

You can do this regardless of your situation in life. Some of the best companies were built by people at the "wrong age" and with the "wrong background." If these people can do it, you can too.

- Ralph Lauren dropped out of school to join the army and then worked as a clerk at Brooks Brothers. He started his fashion line, and is now worth $6.4 billion.
- Don Won Chang moved to America and his first job was as a gas station attendant. He founded Forever 21 and is now worth $5.4 billion.
- John Paul Dejoria was in foster care as a child and lived in his car while selling shampoo door to door. He's the founder of Patrón tequila and the Paul Mitchell line of hair products. Today, he's worth $3.2 billion.
- Howard Schultz grew up in a housing complex for the poor in New York City. He's the CEO of Starbucks and worth $2.9 billion.
- American author, financial advisor, motivational speaker, and television host Suze Orman was a waitress until the age of 30. Now she's worth $25 million.
- Manoj Bhargava was a taxi driver until the age of 30. He then went on to launch the 5-Hour Energy drink and is

worth over $1.5 billion.

Don't make excuses. Keep pushing yourself and always continue learning.

Hungry for more knowledge?

There are so many great books out there around startups, growth, digital marketing and launching a product. Consider this list for your continued education:

What to Read

- *The Viral Startup by Andrew Chen*
- *Traction by Gabriel Weinberg*
- *Lean Analytics by Ben Yoskovitz and Alistar Croll*
- *The Viral Loop by Adam Penenberg*
- *Launch by Jeff Walker*
- *Growth Engines by Sean Ellis*
- *Hooked by Nir Eyal*
- *The Ultimate Sales Machine by Chet Holmes*
- *What Great Brands Do by Denise Lee Yohn*
- *Hacking Growth by Morgan Brown and Sean Ellis*
- GrowthHackers.com
- Paul Graham's Essays blog
- Neil Patel's blog
- First Round Capital Review
- Rob Sobers blog

What to Watch

- How to Start a Startup: Alex Schultz, head of growth at Facebook
- Noah Kagan's YouTube Channel
- Marketing Hell Week by 500 Startups on YouTube
- Conversion Funnels by ClickMinded (video course)

Podcasts to Listen To

- Startup Grind
- The Growth Show
- Seeking Wisdom
- Growth Everywhere
- Traction by NextView
- a16z Podcast
- The Startup Chat
- Startups for the Rest of Us

The secret to growth is not uncovering some new tactic or hack. It's having a product or service that people love, and understanding the customer so well that you know how to speak to them and where to speak to them. It's about being disciplined and focused in your pursuit for sustainable growth.

The best growth strategies don't necessarily come from the smartest marketers. They come from the relentless founders or marketers who truly understand their customer the best. If you focus on that, **then you're starting growth the right way.**

About the Author

Jim Huffman is the founder of the growth agency GrowthHit. He's grown and launched three startups that have been featured by *The Wall Street Journal*, *TODAY*, *Forbes*, *TechCrunch*, *GQ* and *Wired*. Huffman grew one startup to over 100,000 email subscribers in six months and $3 million in sales in 24 months. He scaled another online business to 3 million impressions per month in under 18 months.

Currently, Huffman is overseeing marketing for an VC-backed ecommerce brand that has 100,000 members and does over seven figures in monthly sales. He is a Techstars growth mentor and teaches digital marketing courses at General Assembly. He is also a marketing instructor for the ANA (Association of National Advertisers) and has advised brands like Mattel, FedEx, Sephora and Clorox.

Printed in Great Britain
by Amazon